Exquisite Modular Origami

Meenakshi Mukerji

To my family, friends and fans

Acknowledgements

First of all I would like to thank those who contributed to this book. I would like to thank Dennis Walker for granting me permission to publish the diagrams for the Compound of Five Octahedra (page 18) which is my design inspired by his design. Thanks to Maria Sinayskaya and Ekaterina Lukesheva for contributing to this book their beautiful designs Etna Kusudama (page 58) and Helica Kusudama (page 60) respectively. Thanks to Maria also goes for diagram testing. Ekaterina, Maria and Dennis have also contributed model photos which have been credited below. Thanks to Priti Hansia for proof reading. Thanks to Vinita Singhal for helping me with book production. I would also like to thank all those who constantly encourage me to come up with new designs and to write more books. I wish to thank the fans of my website http://www.origamee.net for their continued support and enthusiasm. A final note of thanks goes to everyone in my family as well as my friends over here in the US, in India and around the world for providing me with so much inspiration.

Photo Credits

Unless otherwise mentioned, all design, folding and photos are by the author.

Cover Photos:
Top Row: Flower Star (folding and photo by Ekaterina Lukasheva); Dimpled Model with Curves; Etna Kusudama (design, folding and photo by Maria Sinayskaya).
Middle Row: Corolla; Star Flower (folding and photo by Maria Sinayskaya); Daffodils.
Bottom Row: Pinwheel Dodecahedron; Compound of Five Octahedra; Helica Kusudama (design, folding and photo by Ekaterina Lukasheva).

Back Cover Photos:
Top Row: Star Flower Variation; Corolla Star (folding and photo by Maria Sinayskaya); Dimpled Model with Flowers.
Bottom Row: Dimpled Model with Curls and Color Change; Zinnia Star; Vortex Dodecahedron.

Photo on Title Page:
Alternate Assembly of Zinnia Star (folding and photo by Dennis Walker).

Photos on Page 12:
Pinwheel and Vortex Dodecahedron Variations.

Photo on Page 17:
Super Simple Greater Stellated Dodecahedron.

Photos on Page 44:
30 and 12 Unit Assemblies of Zinnia.

Photos on Page 62:
Top Row: 12-unit assemblies of Star Flower and Corolla.
Middle Row: Flower Star Variation and Etna Variation.
Bottom Row: Super Simple "Stellated" Cuboctahedron; Unbloomed Helica Kusudama (folding and photo by Ekaterina Lukasheva).

Contents

Preface

This is my fourth book on the subject of modular origami in almost as many years. The warm reception of my previous books, the ever increasing interest in origami around the world, and a flurry of new designs that raided my head, have prompted me to author yet another book. After publishing three full-color origami books I thought of doing an inexpensive grayscale book to make it accessible to a wider range of audience. Origami diagrams in grayscale convey almost as much as those in color. The two sides of paper can be represented by white and gray. The models presented in this book are mostly brand new designs, previously published only in origami periodicals.

Though lot of modular origami designers claim that their models need no glue or avoid the subject altogether, it turns out that a fair number of these models could use some glue even to be handled gently, let alone regular handling. With time I have slowly distanced myself from models requiring glue and folded only those with moderately strong locks. In the same token, my own designs have shifted towards stronger locking for the modules, making glue redundant. Not that there is anything wrong with glue but it is definitely a no-no for origami in its pure form.

The first few pages of the book contain origami basics and other material that must be included in any modular origami book for it to be complete. If you are already familiar with these basics, please feel free to skip ahead. I have provided polyhedron charts for referencing during the model assembly phase. Folding tips, types of paper and other material important to folding origami, particularly modular origami, have been discussed.

I begin with my Super Simple Isosceles Triangle Unit. This unit is so simple that several other people have arrived at the same design independently. Next, I have a Compound of Five Octahedra inspired by Dennis Walker of the UK. There are enhanced Sonobe type models which lock like the Sonobe units but have some extra folds to form patterns (Corolla, Zinnia, Star Flower and variation). The rest of the models in this book can be broadly categorized into blintzed fish base models (Daffodils and Dimpled Models), decorated dodecahedra (Pinwheel, Vortex and variations), and decorated stars (Flower Star, Zinnia Star and Corolla Star). Also included are two models by guests Ekaterina Lukasheva and Maria Sinayskaya, both of Russia. They are prolific designers and it is my privilege to introduce their work Helica and Etna Kusudamas respectively.

The diagrams in this book follow standard origami symbols. The language of origami diagramming is very powerful and can be attributed mostly to origami master Akira Yoshizawa. Although written descriptions are generally provided with the diagrams, they are mostly quite redundant except for certain special circumstances. To keep the diagrams simple and neat I have refrained from showing layers except when necessary. Photographs of all models are presented. Color model photos are on the cover and grayscale ones are all across the book.

This book is meant for audiences 12 years of age and older, with or without a mathematical background. You will enjoy the book irrespective of your folding level, particularly if you are a modular origami lover. Sometimes the units or modules separately may seem quite mundane, but the assembled finished model is always like a pleasant surprise waiting to be cherished at the end. I hope you find hours of enjoyment and relaxation and are tempted to design your own models.

— Cupertino, California, August 2011.

Introduction

The word origami is based on two Japanese words: *oru* (to fold) and *kami* (paper). Although this ancient art of paper folding started in Japan and China, origami is now a household word around the world. Most people have probably folded at least a paper boat or an airplane in their lifetime. Origami has evolved immensely in the present times and is much more than a handful of traditional models. Modular origami, origami sculptures, and origami tessellations are but some of the newer forms of the art. The method of designing models has also evolved. While some models are designed the old fashioned way using mostly imagination and by trial and error, others are designed with complex mathematical algorithms using the computer.

Modular origami, as the name implies, involves assembling several, usually identical, modules or units to form one finished model. While an understanding of mathematics is useful in designing these models, it is not crucial for merely following instructions to construct them. I think that even though mathematics may not be one's strong point, one can still construct these models and perhaps the process might impart a deeper appreciation for the mathematical principles involved. Like any multi-stepped task it requires patience, diligence and a bit of practice. It is always a pleasure to see the finished model at the end, the outcome is often greatly different than the individual parts would have initially suggested. Aesthetics and mathematics brilliantly come together in these wonderful modular origami structures to satisfy our many senses.

Modular origami can be fit relatively easily into one's busy schedule if one can be a bit organized. Unlike many other art forms, long uninterrupted stretches of time are not required. This makes it a perfect artistic endeavor given the hectic, fast paced life we all lead. Upon mastering one unit which usually doesn't take long, several more can be folded anywhere anytime, including the short breaks between other chores. When the units are all folded, the final assembly can also be done slowly over time. Modular origami is great for folding during the inevitable waits at airports, doctor's offices or even on long flights. Just remember to carry your paper, diagrams and maybe a box for the finished units that are 3D. It's best to assemble the model at home because finished models are difficult to carry.

Assembly of the units that comprise a model may at first seem very puzzling to the novice, or even downright impossible. But understanding certain aspects can considerably simplify the process. First, one must determine whether a unit is a face unit, an edge unit, or a vertex unit, i.e., whether a unit identifies with a face, an edge or a vertex respectively, of a polyhedron. Face units are the easiest to identify. There are only a few known vertex units, e.g., David Mitchell's Electra [Mit00] and Ravi Apte's Universal Vertex Module [Tan02]. Most modular units tend to be edge units. For edge units there is a second step involved - one must identify which part of the unit, which is far from looking like an edge, actually maps to the edge of a polyhedron. Although it may appear perplexing at first, on closer look one may find that it is not an impossible task. Once the identifications are made and the folder can see through the maze of superficial designs and perceive the unit as a face, an edge, or a vertex, assembly becomes simple. It is then just a matter of following the structure of the underlying polyhedron to assemble the units.

Origami Tips, Tools and Paper

Origami Tips

❖ Use paper of the same thickness and texture for all units. This ensures that the look and strength of the finished models will be uniform. Virtually any paper from printer paper to gift-wrap may be used to fold origami.

❖ Make sure that the grain of the paper is oriented the same way for all your units. To determine the grain of the paper, gently bend paper both horizontally and vertically. The grain of the paper is said to lie along the direction that offers less resistance.

❖ Accuracy is particularly crucial in modular origami, so your folds need to be as accurate as possible. Only then will the finished models look symmetric, neat and appealing.

❖ It is advisable to fold a trial unit before folding the real units. In some models the finished unit is much smaller than the starting paper size, while in others this is not the case. Making a trial unit will give you an idea of what the size of the finished units—and hence a finished model—might be, starting with a certain paper size. It will also give you an idea about the paper properties and whether the paper type selected is suitable for the model you are making.

❖ After you have determined your paper size and type, procure all the paper you need for the model before starting. If you do not have all the paper at the beginning, you may discover, as has been my experience, that you are not able to find more paper of the same kind to finish your model.

❖ If a step looks difficult, looking ahead to the next step often helps immensely. This is because the execution of a current step results in what is diagrammed in the next step.

❖ Assembly aids such as miniature clothespins or paper clips are often advisable, especially for beginners. Some assemblies simply need them whether you are a beginner or not. These pins or clips may be removed as the assembly progresses or upon completion of the model.

❖ During assembly, putting together the last few units, especially the very last one, can be challenging. During those times, remember that it is paper you are working with and not metal! Paper is flexible and can be bent or flexed for ease of assembly.

❖ After completion, hold the model in both hands and compress gently to make sure that all the tabs are securely and completely in their corresponding pockets. Finish by working your fingers around the ball.

❖ Use templates in unusual folding such as folding into thirds, to reduce unwanted creases. The templates in turn can be created using origami methods.

❖ Procure a minimal set of basic handy tools listed on the next page. These tools assist in sizing paper, making neat and crisp creases, curling paper, and assembling models.

Origami Tools

❖ Creasing Tools: The most basic tool that is used in origami is a bone folder. It allows making precise and crisp creases and prevents your nails from being sore when folding excessively. Substitutes might be credit cards or other similar objects.

❖ Cutting Tools: Although cutting is prohibited in pure origami, cutting tools are required for the initial sizing of the paper. A great cutting tool would be a paper guillotine but it is bulky and may not be readily accessible to all people. I find a portable photo trimmer with replaceable blades to be a great substitute. They are inexpensive and easily carried anywhere. Scissors may be used but it is very difficult to get straight cuts.

❖ Curling Tools: Many origami models involve curling. Chop sticks, knitting needles, screwdrivers, or similar objects such as narrow pencils work well for curling paper.

❖ Other Tools: Miniature clothespins may be used during model assembly as temporary aids to hold two adjacent units together. The clothespins may be removed as the assembly progresses or after completion. Tweezers may be used to access hard to reach places or for folding paper that becomes too small to maneuver with fingers.

Origami Paper

Origami can be folded from practically any type of paper. But every model has some paper that works best for it and mostly experience can tell which one. Some models might require sturdy paper while some others might require paper that creases softly. Origami made from company logo paper makes good gifts for bosses and colleagues and discarded sheet music can be used for folding gifts for music teachers (see example on pages 17 and 62). I have extensively used recycled/reused paper for making some of my models. For finished models in which the reverse side of the paper is not visible, one can use flyer paper that is printed only on one side. The following is a list of readily available origami paper.

❖ Kami: This is the most readily available origami paper. It is solidly colored on one side and white on the other.

❖ Duo: Paper that is one color on one side and a different color on the other.

❖ Printer paper: Paper, white or colored, that is commonly used in home or office computer printers.

❖ Mono: These papers have the same color on both sides. Printer paper is an example of mono paper. You may also find mono paper in kami strength.

❖ Harmony paper: Paper that has some harmonious pattern formed by various colors blending into one another. When used it can have a dramatic effect on some models.

❖ Chiyogami: Origami paper with patterns, usually small, printed on it.

❖ Washi: Handmade Japanese paper with plant fiber in the pulp that gives it texture.

❖ Foil backed paper: These have metallic foil on one side and paper on the other side.

Origami Symbols and Bases

This is a list of commonly used origami symbols and bases.

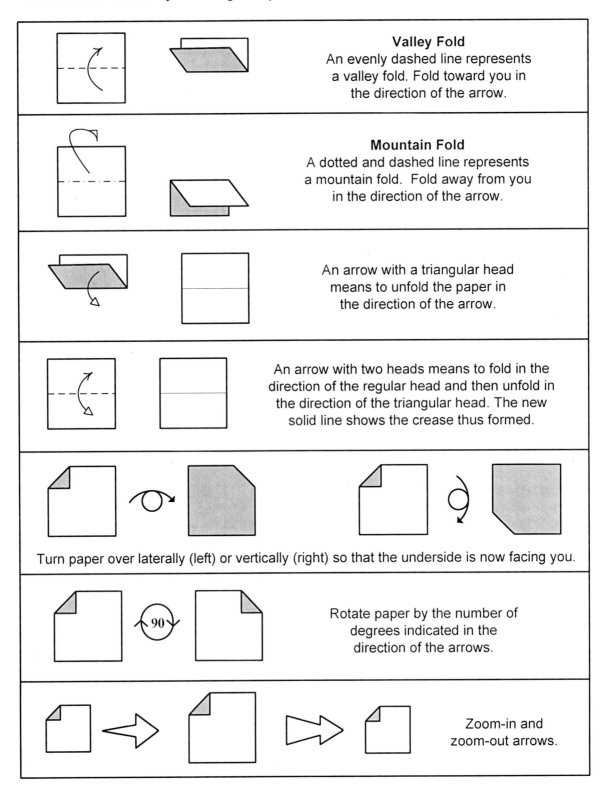

	Valley Fold An evenly dashed line represents a valley fold. Fold toward you in the direction of the arrow.
	Mountain Fold A dotted and dashed line represents a mountain fold. Fold away from you in the direction of the arrow.
	An arrow with a triangular head means to unfold the paper in the direction of the arrow.
	An arrow with two heads means to fold in the direction of the regular head and then unfold in the direction of the triangular head. The new solid line shows the crease thus formed.

Turn paper over laterally (left) or vertically (right) so that the underside is now facing you.

Rotate paper by the number of degrees indicated in the direction of the arrows.

Zoom-in and zoom-out arrows.

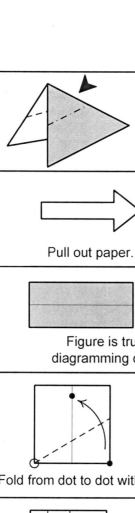
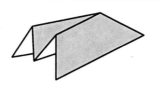

**Reverse Fold or
Inside Reverse Fold**
Push in the direction of the
arrow to arrive at the result.

Pull out paper.

Equal lengths.

Equal angles.

Figure is truncated for
diagramming convenience.

Repeat once, twice, or as
many times as indicated by
the tail of the arrow.

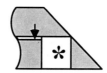
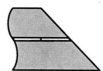

Fold from dot to dot with the circled point as pivot.

✱ : Tuck in opening underneath.

Fold repeatedly to arrive
at the result.

Pleat Fold

An alternate mountain and valley fold to form a pleat. Two examples are shown.

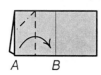
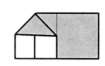

A   B

Squash Fold
Turn paper to the right along the
valley fold while making the mountain
crease such that *A* finally lies on *B*.

Cupboard Fold
First fold and unfold the centerfold, also called
the *book-fold*, then valley fold the left and right
edges to the center like cupboard doors.

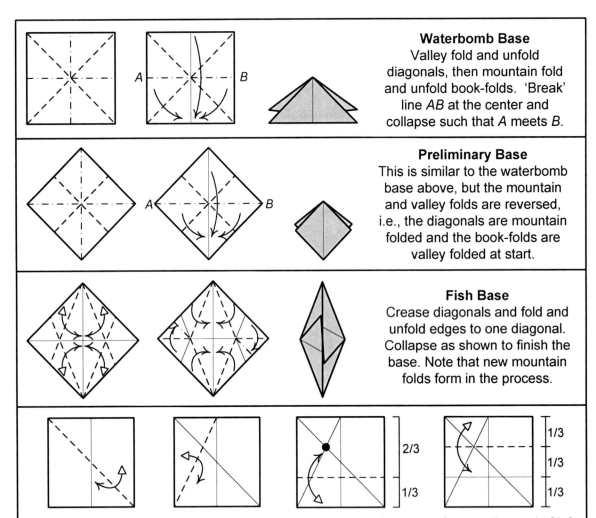

Waterbomb Base
Valley fold and unfold diagonals, then mountain fold and unfold book-folds. 'Break' line AB at the center and collapse such that A meets B.

Preliminary Base
This is similar to the waterbomb base above, but the mountain and valley folds are reversed, i.e., the diagonals are mountain folded and the book-folds are valley folded at start.

Fish Base
Crease diagonals and fold and unfold edges to one diagonal. Collapse as shown to finish the base. Note that new mountain folds form in the process.

Folding A Square into Thirds: Crease book-fold and one diagonal. Crease diagonal of left rectangle to find 1/3 point. Bring bottom edge to this point and top edge to new line.

Pinwheel Dodecahedron Variation (pg 33) and Vortex Dodecahedron Variation (pg 37).

Platonic, Archimedean and Kepler-Poinsot Solids

Shown below are sets of polyhedra commonly referenced during origami constructions.

The Platonic solids, named after the ancient Greek philosopher Plato (428-348 BC), also called the regular solids, are convex polyhedra bound by faces that are congruent regular convex polygons. The same numbers of faces meet at each vertex. There are exactly five.

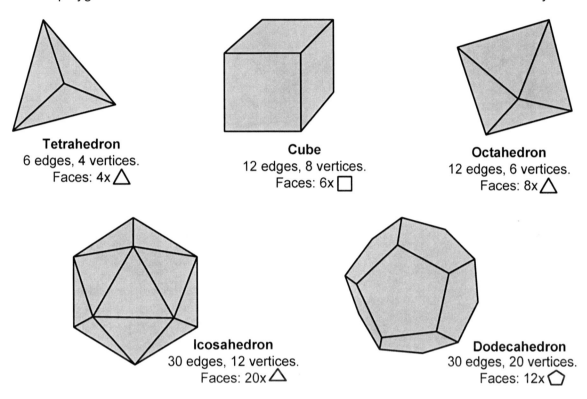

Tetrahedron
6 edges, 4 vertices.
Faces: 4x △

Cube
12 edges, 8 vertices.
Faces: 6x □

Octahedron
12 edges, 6 vertices.
Faces: 8x △

Icosahedron
30 edges, 12 vertices.
Faces: 20x △

Dodecahedron
30 edges, 20 vertices.
Faces: 12x ⬠

The Archimedean solids, named after Archimedes (287-212 BC), are semi-regular convex polyhedra bound by two or more types of regular convex polygons meeting in identical vertices. They are distinct from the Platonic solids which are composed of a single type of polygon meeting at identical vertices. Shown here are 8 of the 13 Archimedean solids. Those not shown are the Snub Dodecahedron, Truncated Tetrahedron, Truncated Dodecahedron, Great Rhombicosidodecahedron and Great Rhombicuboctahedron.

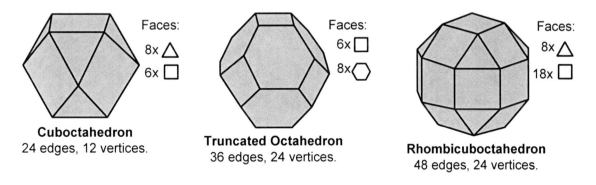

Faces:
8x △
6x □

Cuboctahedron
24 edges, 12 vertices.

Faces:
6x □
8x ⬡

Truncated Octahedron
36 edges, 24 vertices.

Faces:
8x △
18x □

Rhombicuboctahedron
48 edges, 24 vertices.

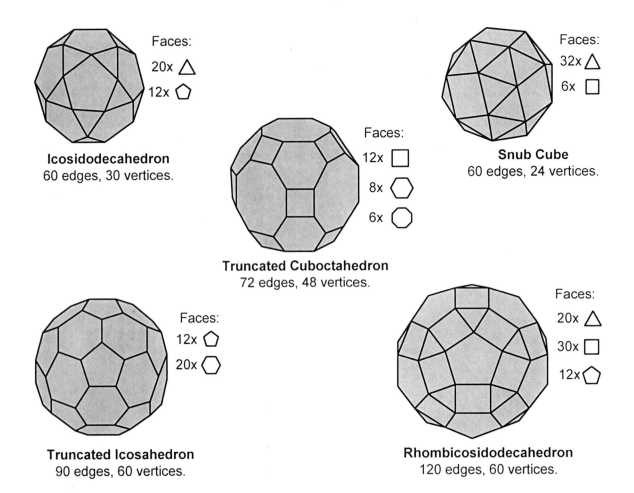

Icosidodecahedron
60 edges, 30 vertices.

Faces:
20x △
12x ⬠

Truncated Cuboctahedron
72 edges, 48 vertices.

Faces:
12x ☐
8x ⬡
6x ⯃

Snub Cube
60 edges, 24 vertices.

Faces:
32x △
6x ☐

Truncated Icosahedron
90 edges, 60 vertices.

Faces:
12x ⬠
20x ⬡

Rhombicosidodecahedron
120 edges, 60 vertices.

Faces:
20x △
30x ☐
12x ⬠

The Kepler-Poinsot solids, named after Johannes Kepler and Louis Poinsot (17th -19th century), are four regular concave polyhedra with intersecting facial planes. These can be obtained by stellating Platonic solids. Only two of the four are shown below. The two not shown are the Great Dodecahedron and the Great Icosahedron.

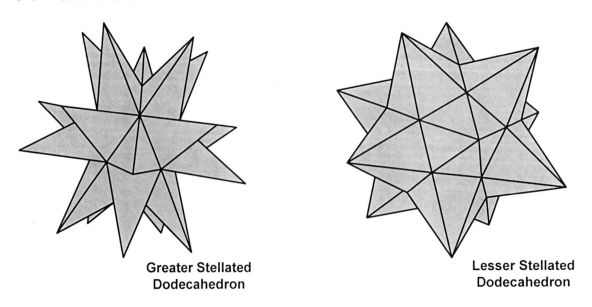

Greater Stellated Dodecahedron

Lesser Stellated Dodecahedron

Super Simple Isosceles Triangle Unit

(Created June 2001)

As the name implies this is a very simple unit. So naturally, it has been discovered independently by many. This model will make one familiar with assembling the Kepler-Poinsot solids discussed previously, and the experience can form the basis of many of my origami designs presented later in the book. Note that it is possible to build a "stellated" version of any other polyhedron with this unit. Here I use the word stellated in a loose sense and not in a true mathematical sense, merely meaning that the faces of a chosen polyhedron could be extended to pyramids imagining the faces as bases, thus forming spikes of a star. However, the two stellations of a dodecahedron constructed next are the true stellated dodecahedra.

Make a template by folding a square into thirds. Use the method explained at the end of the section *Origami Symbols & Bases.* Use this template for performing Step 1 below.

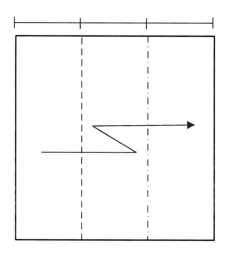

1. Pleat fold into thirds.

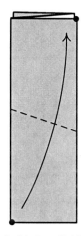

2. Valley fold to match dots.

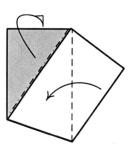

3. Valley and mountain fold as shown.

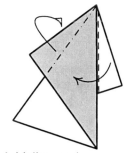

4. Valley and mountain fold as shown.

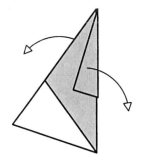

5. Unfold all to Step 2.

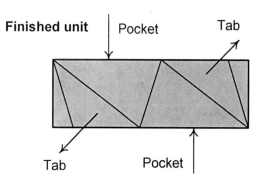

Finished unit   Pocket   Tab

Tab   Pocket

Make 12, 24 or 30 units depending on what polyhedron you want to build.

Assembly

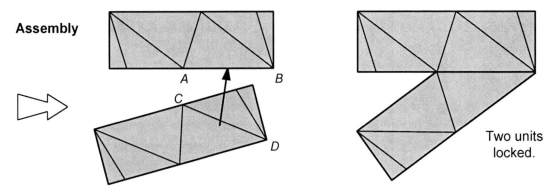

Insert tab into pocket such that *CD* aligns with *AB*.

Two units
locked.

Showing 30-unit Lesser Stellated
Dodecahedral assembly.

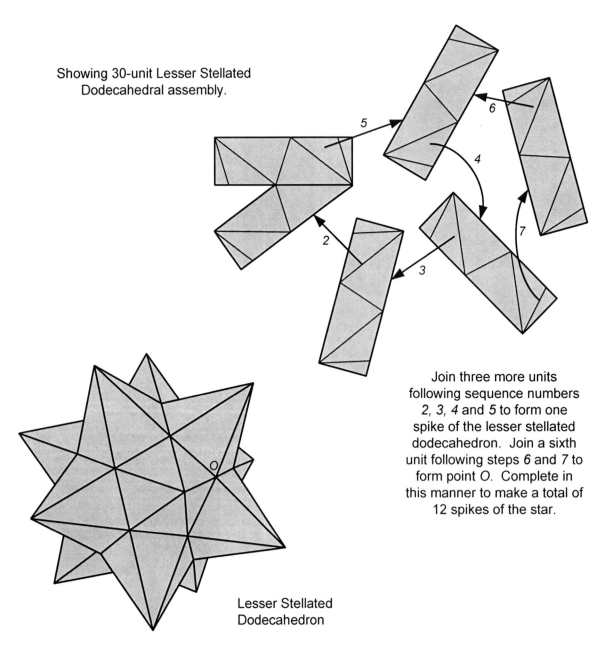

Join three more units
following sequence numbers
2, 3, 4 and *5* to form one
spike of the lesser stellated
dodecahedron. Join a sixth
unit following steps *6* and *7* to
form point *O*. Complete in
this manner to make a total of
12 spikes of the star.

Lesser Stellated
Dodecahedron

Showing 30-unit Greater Stellated Dodecahedral assembly.

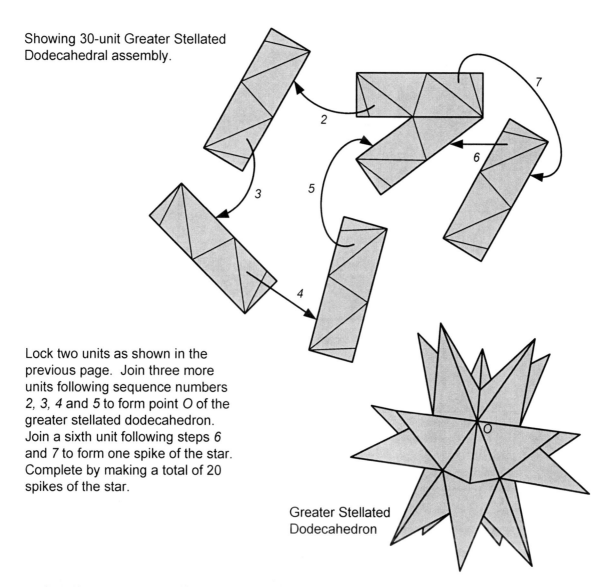

Lock two units as shown in the previous page. Join three more units following sequence numbers *2, 3, 4* and *5* to form point *O* of the greater stellated dodecahedron. Join a sixth unit following steps *6* and *7* to form one spike of the star. Complete by making a total of 20 spikes of the star.

Greater Stellated Dodecahedron

Greater Stellated Docecahedron made with sheet music paper. For photo of a 24-unit "stellated" cuboctahedral assembly, please see page 62.

Compound of Five Octahedra

(Created April 2010)

This model is a 30 unit version of Dennis Walker's 60-unit model. It is also called the third stellation of the icosahedron.

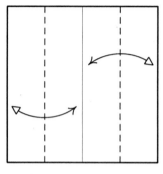

1. Crease book-fold and then cupboard fold and unfold.

2. Mountain fold center.

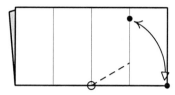

3. With thumb at bottom center pivot point, match dots and crease only the part shown.

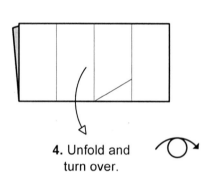

4. Unfold and turn over.

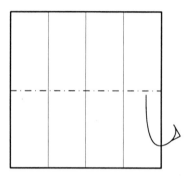

5. Extend the new creases as shown .

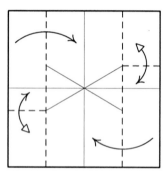

6. Crease the two horizontal lines.

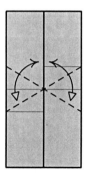

7. Valley fold and unfold to trace creases behind.

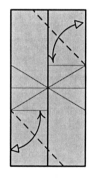

8. Valley fold and unfold the two corners shown.

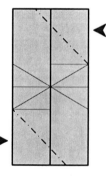

9. Inside reverse fold corners.

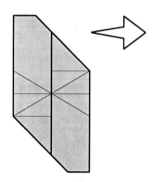

10. Unfold all except the 2 little folds at the corners.

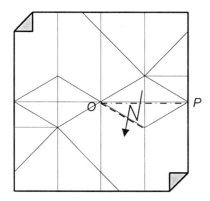

11. Mountain and valley fold as shown.

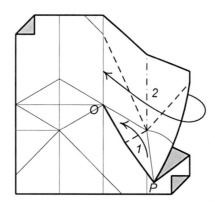

12. Valley fold to bring P to O and the right edge to the book-fold while making the reverse fold of Step 9 reappear.

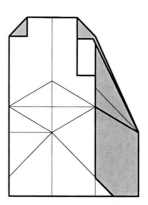

13. The unit is now 3D. Rotate 180°.

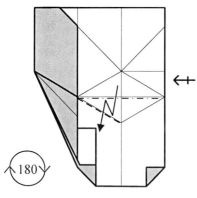

14. Repeat Steps 11 and 12 on right.

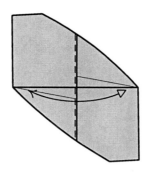

15. Valley fold and unfold firmly along spine.

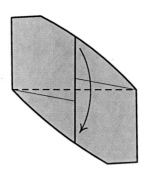

16. Valley fold to flatten unit.

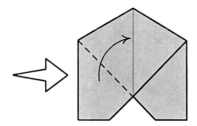

17. Valley fold to form tab.

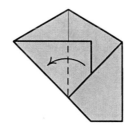

18. Valley fold to form lock.

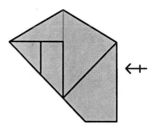

19. Repeat Steps 17 and 18 behind.

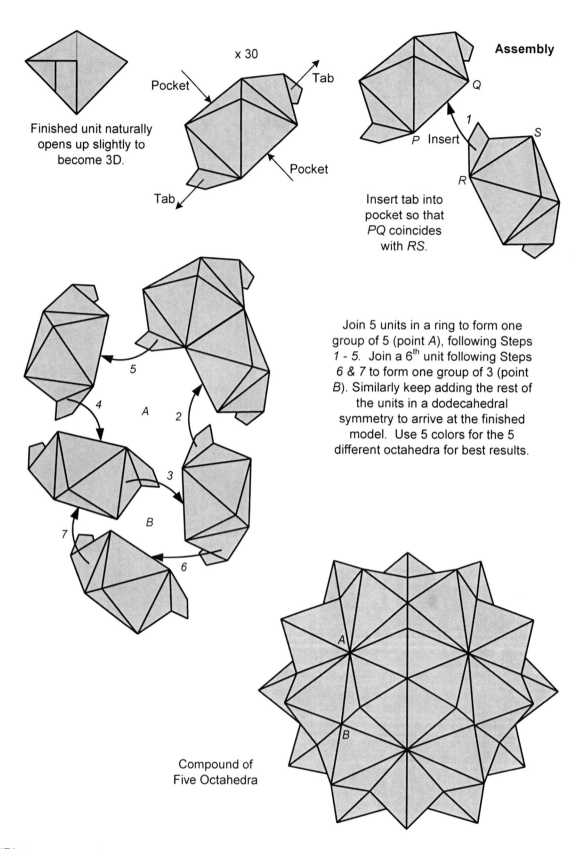

Finished unit naturally
opens up slightly to
become 3D.

x 30

Pocket

Tab

Pocket

Tab

Assembly

Q

P Insert

S

R

Insert tab into
pocket so that
PQ coincides
with *RS*.

Join 5 units in a ring to form one
group of 5 (point *A*), following Steps
1 - 5. Join a 6th unit following Steps
6 & 7 to form one group of 3 (point
B). Similarly keep adding the rest of
the units in a dodecahedral
symmetry to arrive at the finished
model. Use 5 colors for the 5
different octahedra for best results.

5

4

A

2

3

B

7

6

A

B

Compound of
Five Octahedra

(Photo on cover)

Daffodils

(Created March 2011)

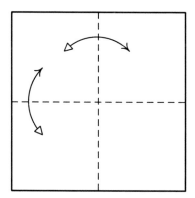

1. Fold and unfold both book-folds.

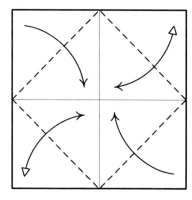

2. Fold corners to center. Unfold the two corners shown.

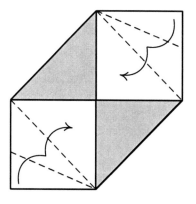

3. Valley fold the two corners repeatedly.

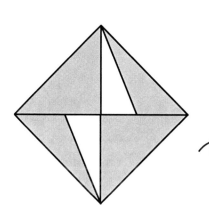

4. Turn over.

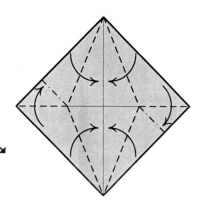

5. Fold like a fish base following the valley and mountain folds.

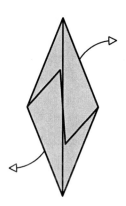

6. Unfold the two flaps behind.

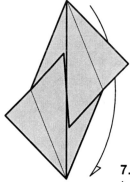

7. Bring top tip to bottom mountain folding back layer only.

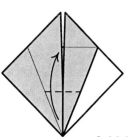

8. Valley fold top flap creasing only where shown.

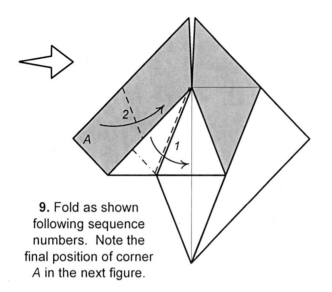

9. Fold as shown following sequence numbers. Note the final position of corner *A* in the next figure.

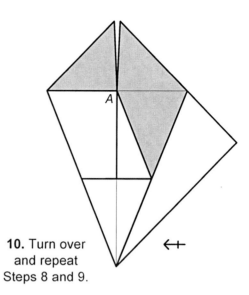

10. Turn over and repeat Steps 8 and 9.

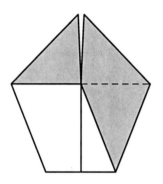

11. <u>Softly</u> bend forward along existing crease.

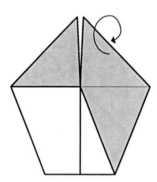

12. Curl the right flap towards you.

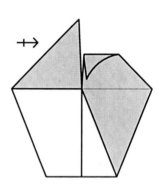

13. Turn over and repeat Steps 11 and 12.

Finished Unit

Assembly

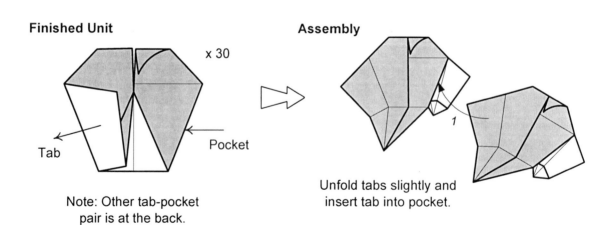

x 30

Tab

Pocket

Note: Other tab-pocket pair is at the back.

Unfold tabs slightly and insert tab into pocket.

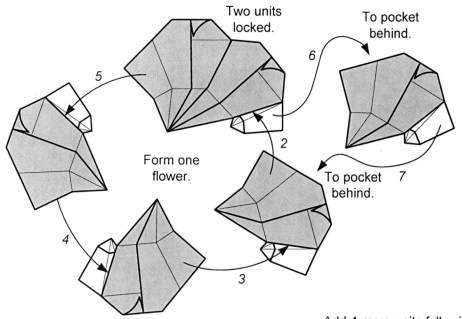

Two units
locked.

To pocket
behind.

6

5

Form one
flower.

2

To pocket
behind.

7

4

3

Add 4 more units following Steps *2-5* to form one flower. Add a sixth unit following Steps *6* and *7* to form one vertex. Continue assembling the rest of the units in this manner to form a total of 12 flowers in a dodecahedral symmetry to finish the model. Note that the bend in the tabs and pockets secure the locking.

Daffodils
(Note: The darker shade is used to distinguish the pentagonal pyramids at the center of the flowers.)

(Photo on cover)

Dimpled Model with Curls

(Created March 2011)

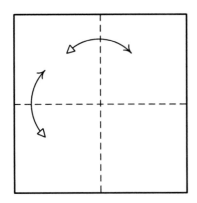

1. Fold and unfold
both book-folds.

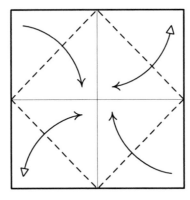

2. Fold corners to center.
Unfold the two corners shown.

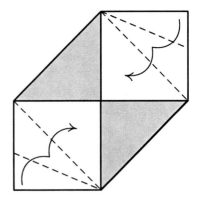

3. Repeatedly valley fold
the two corners as shown.

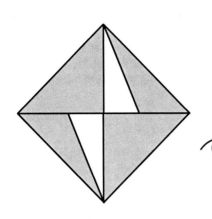

4. Turn over.

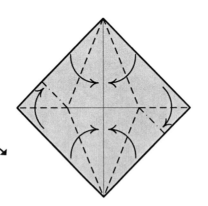

5. Fold like a fish base
following the valley and
mountain folds.

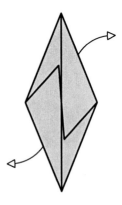

6. Unfold the two
flaps behind.

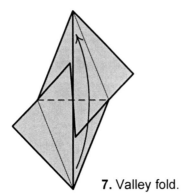

7. Valley fold.

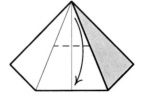

8. Valley fold top
flap creasing only
where shown.

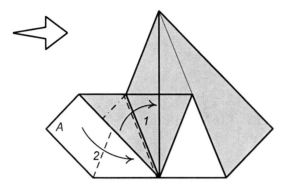

9. Fold as shown following sequence numbers. Note the final position of corner *A* in the next figure.

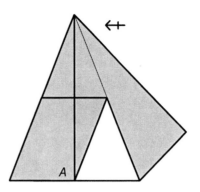

10. Turn over and repeat Steps 8 and 9.

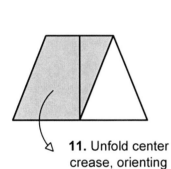

11. Unfold center crease, orienting inner flaps as shown in the next figure.

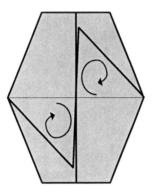

12. Curl flaps towards you.

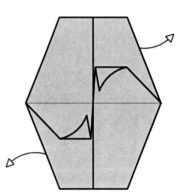

13. Unfold flaps at back slightly to finish unit.

Finished Unit

x 30

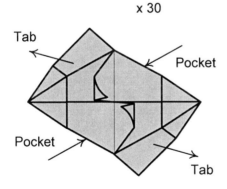

Tab

Pocket

Pocket

Tab

Assembly

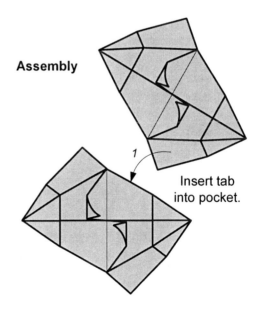

1

Insert tab into pocket.

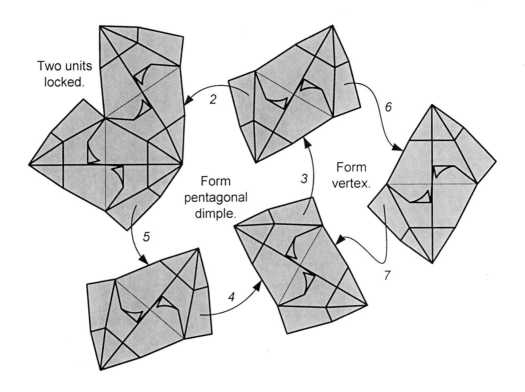

Two units locked.

Form pentagonal dimple.

Form vertex.

2

3

4

5

6

7

Add 4 more units following Steps 2-5 to form one pentagonal dimple. Add a sixth unit following Steps 6 and 7 to form one vertex. Continue assembling the rest of the units in this manner to form a total of 12 dimpled faces in a dodecahedral symmetry to finish the model. Note that the bends in the tabs and pockets strengthen the joints.

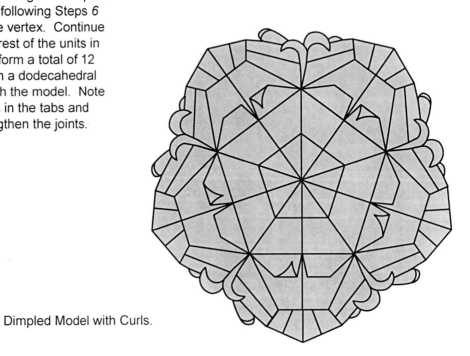

Dimpled Model with Curls.

Dimpled Model with Flowers

(Created March 2011)

Start by completing up to Step 11 of previous model, Dimpled Model with Curls.

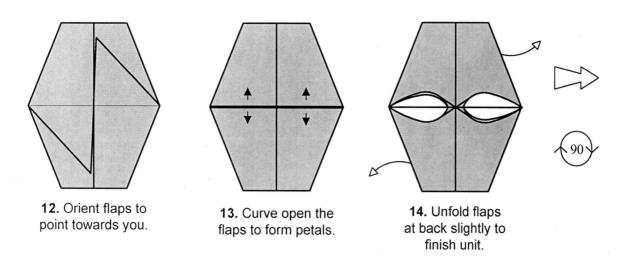

12. Orient flaps to point towards you.

13. Curve open the flaps to form petals.

14. Unfold flaps at back slightly to finish unit.

Finished Unit   x 30

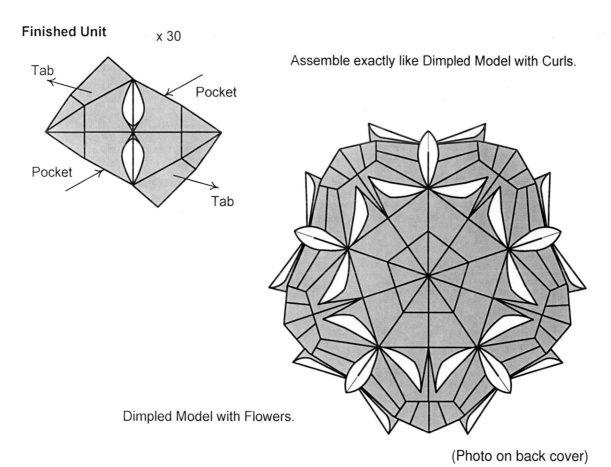

Tab

Pocket

Pocket

Tab

Assemble exactly like Dimpled Model with Curls.

Dimpled Model with Flowers.

(Photo on back cover)

Dimpled Model with Curves

(Created March 2011)

Start by completing up to Step 11 of Dimpled Model with Curls on page 24.

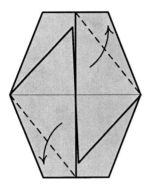 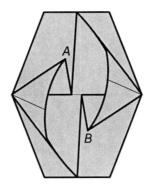 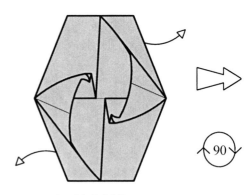

12. Valley fold, top flaps only.

13. Reinforce curves and curl the corners *A* and *B* inwards or outwards.

14. Unfold flaps at back slightly to finish unit.

Finished Unit　x 30

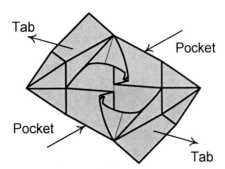

Tab

Pocket

Pocket

Tab

Assemble exactly like Dimpled Model with Curls.

Dimpled Model with Curves.

(Photo on cover)

Dimpled Model with Color Change

(Created March 2011)

The Dimpled Models with Curls as well as with Curves can also be made with color change. Just replace Steps 2-4 with Steps 2'-4' to get the color change effect. Do the rest of the steps as the original models.

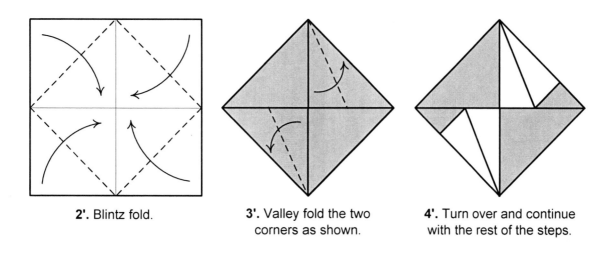

2'. Blintz fold.

3'. Valley fold the two corners as shown.

4'. Turn over and continue with the rest of the steps.

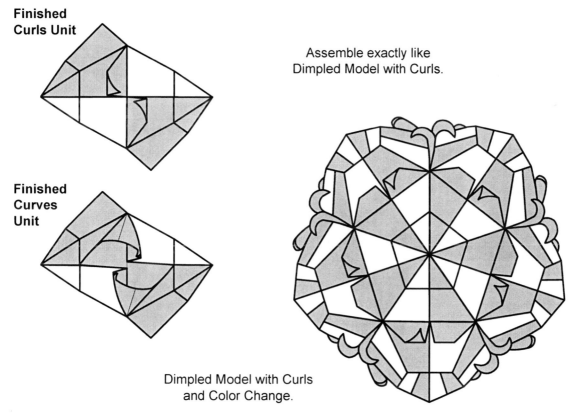

Finished Curls Unit

Finished Curves Unit

Assemble exactly like Dimpled Model with Curls.

Dimpled Model with Curls and Color Change.

(Photo on back cover)

Pinwheel Dodecahedron

(Created November 2010)

Make a template by folding a square into thirds using the method explained at the end of the section *Origami Symbols & Bases*. Use this template for performing Step 1 below.

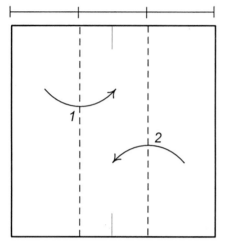

1. Pinch ends of book-fold and fold into thirds following the number sequence.

2. Valley fold top layer only.

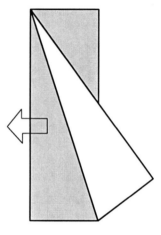

3. Pull bottom flap out to top and repeat Step 2.

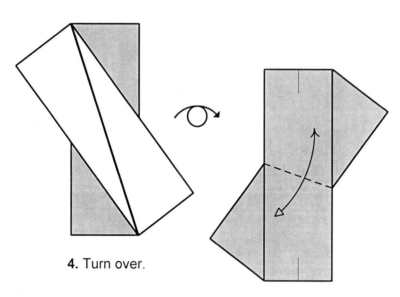

4. Turn over.

5. Valley fold and unfold.

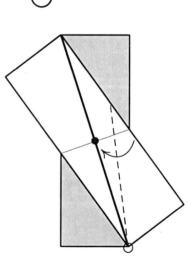

6. With swivel point at bottom corner of right flap bring right edge to center.

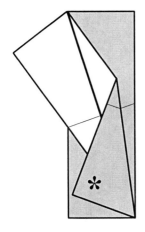

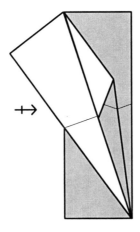

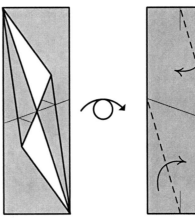

7. Tuck flap underneath.

8. Repeat Steps 6 and 7 on left.

9. Turn over.

10. Valley fold as shown.

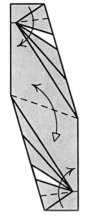

11. Valley fold tips and reinforce fold at center through all layers.

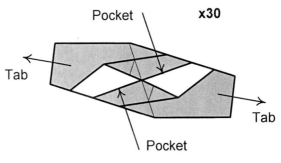

Finished unit

Pocket

x30

Tab

Pocket

Tab

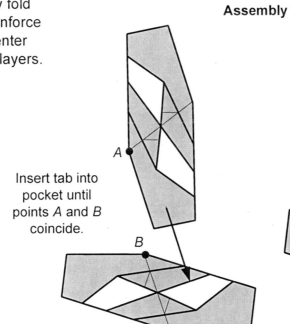

Assembly

Insert tab into pocket until points *A* and *B* coincide.

A

B

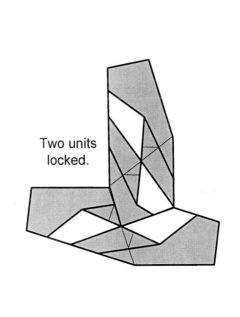

Two units locked.

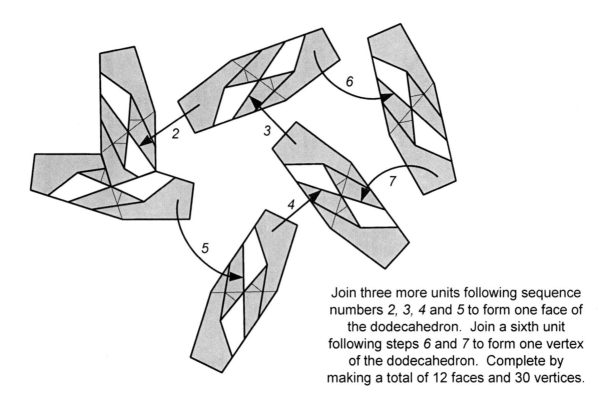

Join three more units following sequence numbers *2*, *3*, *4* and *5* to form one face of the dodecahedron. Join a sixth unit following steps *6* and *7* to form one vertex of the dodecahedron. Complete by making a total of 12 faces and 30 vertices.

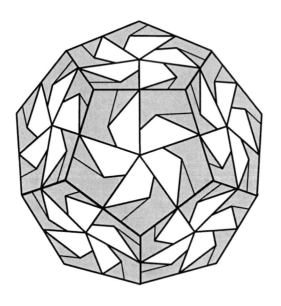

Pinwheel Dodecahedron (left). Showing one face of the dodecahedron in reverse coloring (bottom).

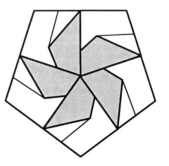

(Photo on cover)

Pinwheel Dodecahedron Variation

(Created November 2010)

This model has smaller pinwheels that do not touch the edges of the dodecahedron.
Start by doing up to Step 5 of Pinwheel Dodecahedron.

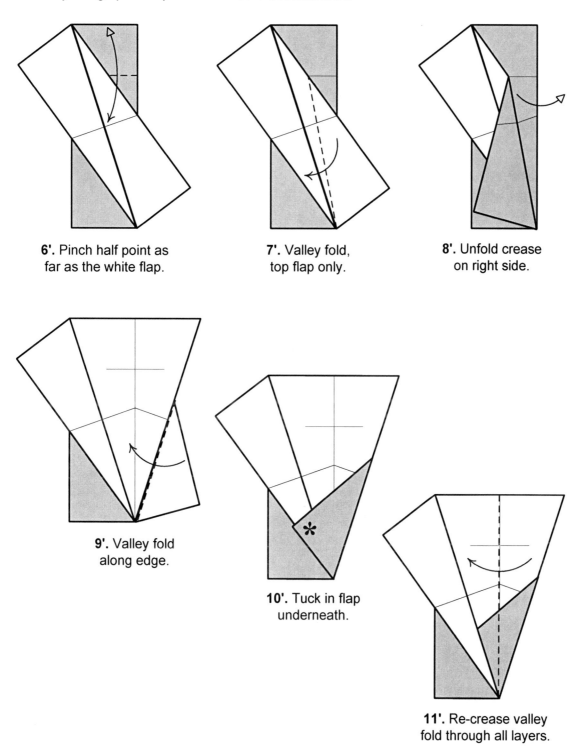

6'. Pinch half point as
far as the white flap.

7'. Valley fold,
top flap only.

8'. Unfold crease
on right side.

9'. Valley fold
along edge.

10'. Tuck in flap
underneath.

11'. Re-crease valley
fold through all layers.

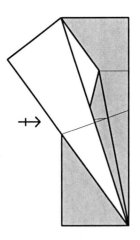 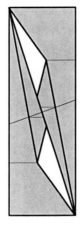

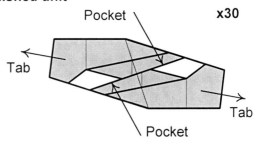

Finished unit

Pocket

x30

Tab

Tab

Pocket

12'. Repeat Steps 6'-11' on the left.

13'. Repeat Steps 9-11 of Pinwheel Dodecahedron to complete unit.

Assemble like Pinwheel Dodecahedron.

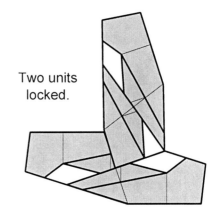

Two units locked.

Pinwheel Dodecahedron Variation (left). Showing one face of the dodecahedron in reverse coloring (bottom).

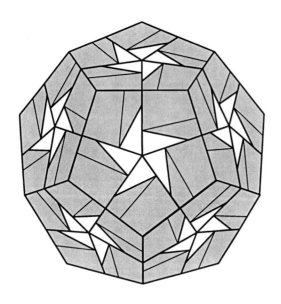

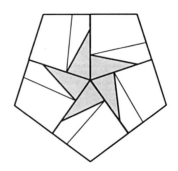

(Photo on page 12)

Vortex Dodecahedron

(Created November 2010)

Make a template by folding a square into thirds using the method explained at the end of the section *Origami Symbols & Bases*. Use this template for performing Step 1 below.

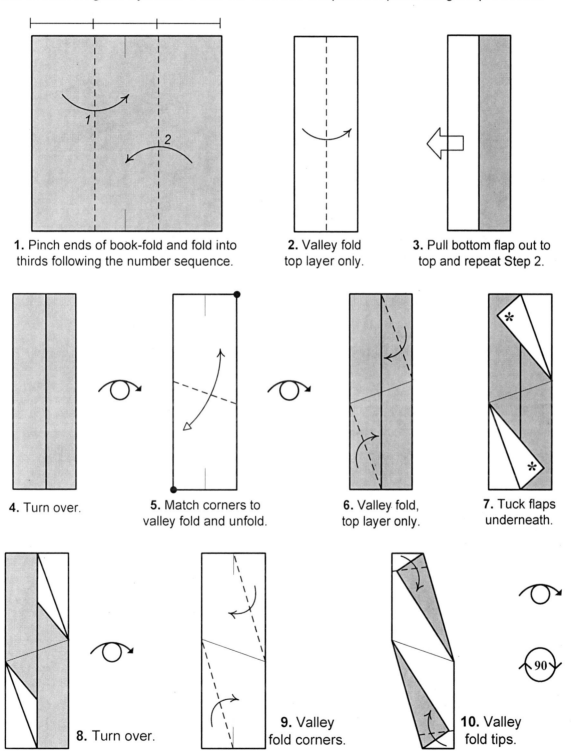

1. Pinch ends of book-fold and fold into thirds following the number sequence.

2. Valley fold top layer only.

3. Pull bottom flap out to top and repeat Step 2.

4. Turn over.

5. Match corners to valley fold and unfold.

6. Valley fold, top layer only.

7. Tuck flaps underneath.

8. Turn over.

9. Valley fold corners.

10. Valley fold tips.

Finished unit

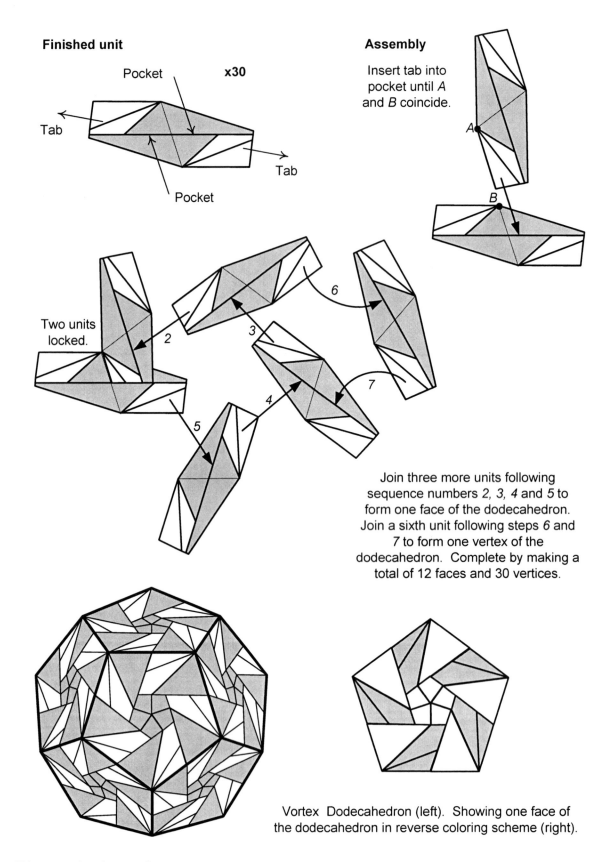

Pocket

x30

Tab

Tab

Pocket

Assembly

Insert tab into pocket until *A* and *B* coincide.

A

B

Two units locked.

2

3

6

4

5

7

Join three more units following sequence numbers *2, 3, 4* and *5* to form one face of the dodecahedron. Join a sixth unit following steps *6* and *7* to form one vertex of the dodecahedron. Complete by making a total of 12 faces and 30 vertices.

Vortex Dodecahedron (left). Showing one face of the dodecahedron in reverse coloring scheme (right).

(Photo on back cover)

Vortex Dodecahedron Variation

(Created November 2010)

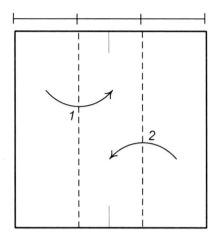

1'. With white side facing you do Steps 1-8 of Vortex Dodecahedron.

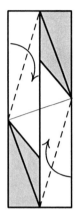

9'. Valley fold, top layer only.

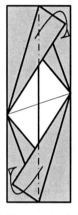

10'. Mountain fold to tuck underneath.

11'. Do Steps 9 and 10 of Vortex Dodecahedron to complete unit.

Finished unit

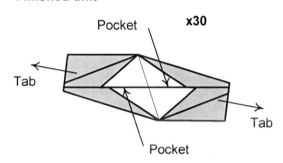

x30

Pocket

Tab

Pocket

Tab

Assemble like Vortex Dodecahedron to complete model.

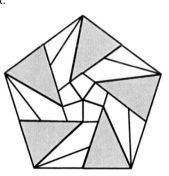

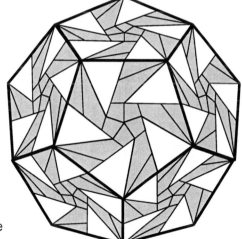

Vortex Dodecahedron Variation (right). Showing one face of the dodecahedron in reverse coloring (above).

(Photo on page 12)

Star Flower

(Created October 2010)

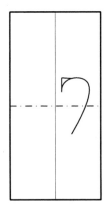

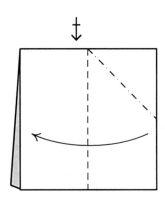

1. Start with 1:2 paper. Valley fold and unfold book-fold and then mountain fold into half.

2. Squash as shown and repeat behind.

3. Valley fold top flap only.

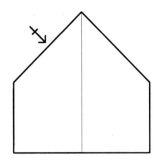

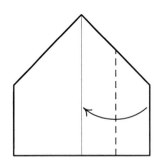

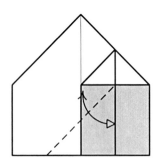

4. Repeat behind.

5. Valley fold, top flap only.

6. Valley fold and unfold, top flap only.

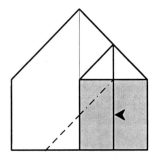

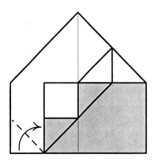

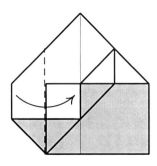

7. Inside reverse fold along crease you just made.

8. Valley fold, top flap only.

9. Valley fold, top flap only.

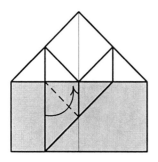

10. Valley fold as shown.

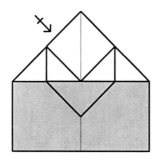

11. Repeat Steps 5-10 behind.

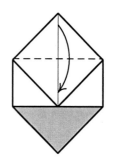

12. Valley fold to crease very firmly.

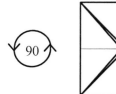

13. Pull tips apart gently to complete the unit.

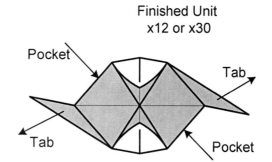

Finished Unit
x12 or x30

Pocket

Tab

Tab

Pocket

Assembly

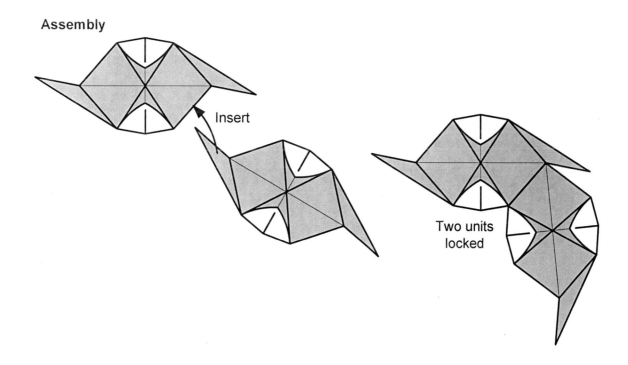

Insert

Two units
locked

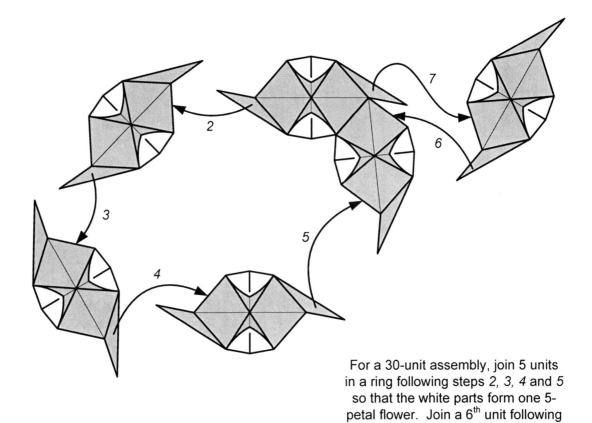

For a 30-unit assembly, join 5 units in a ring following steps *2, 3, 4* and *5* so that the white parts form one 5-petal flower. Join a 6th unit following steps *6* and *7* to form one vertex. Similarly keep adding the rest of the units in a dodecahedral/icosahedral symmetry to arrive at the finished model. For a 12-unit assembly, join 4 units in a ring and complete by following an octahedral symmetry.

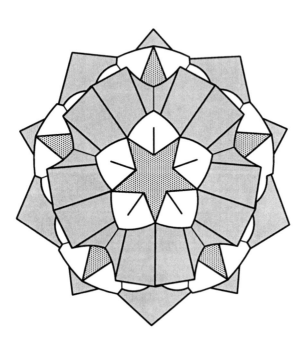

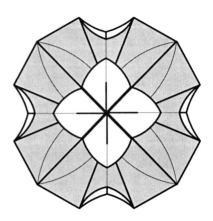

30-unit Star Flower (left) and 12-unit Star Flower (right).

(Photos on cover and page 62)

Star Flower Variation

(Created October 2010)

Start with Step 13 of Star Flower.

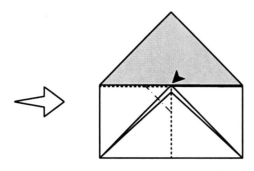
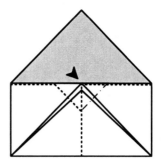

14. The dotted lines show the inside flap in X-ray vision. Inside reverse fold corner slightly at desired location.

15. Repeat symmetrically on the right flap and finish unit like Star Flower.

Assemble exactly like Star Flower.

Finished Unit
x12 or x30

Pocket

Tab

Tab

Pocket

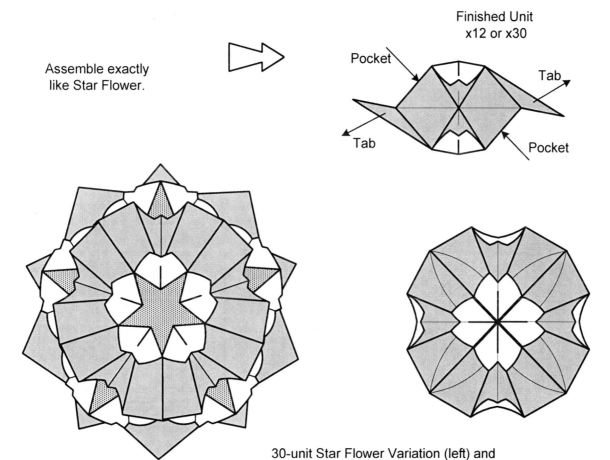

30-unit Star Flower Variation (left) and 12-unit Star Flower Variation (right).

(Photo on back cover)

Zinnia

(Created July 2007)

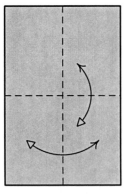

1. Start with 2:3 paper and crease both book-folds.

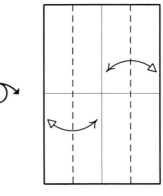

2. Cupboard fold and unfold.

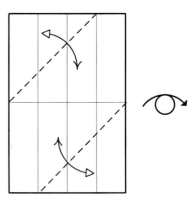

3. Valley fold and unfold.

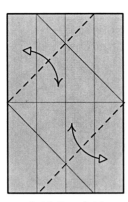

4. Valley fold and unfold.

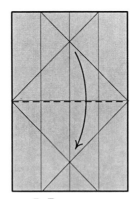

5. Re-crease valley fold.

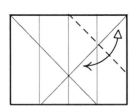

6. Valley fold corner, then unfold all.

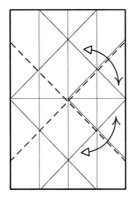

7. Fold and unfold the diagonals shown, using creases made in Step 6.

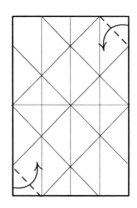

8. Valley fold corners shown.

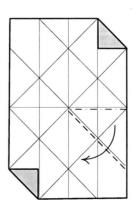

9. Valley and mountain fold pre-existing creases.

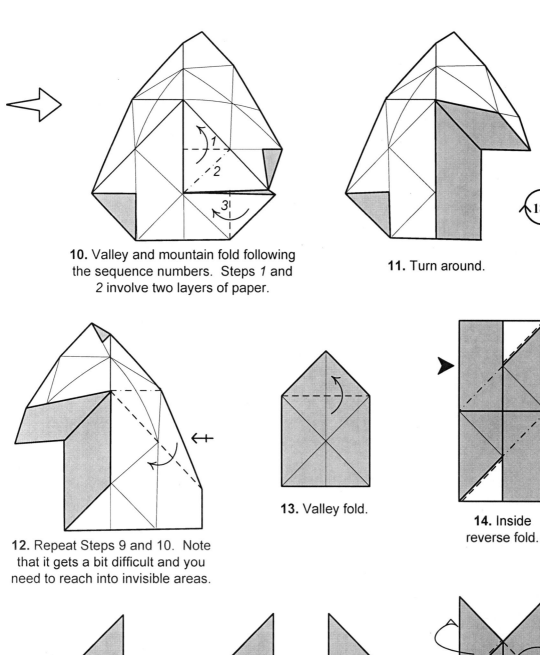

10. Valley and mountain fold following the sequence numbers. Steps *1* and *2* involve two layers of paper.

11. Turn around.

12. Repeat Steps 9 and 10. Note that it gets a bit difficult and you need to reach into invisible areas.

13. Valley fold.

14. Inside reverse fold.

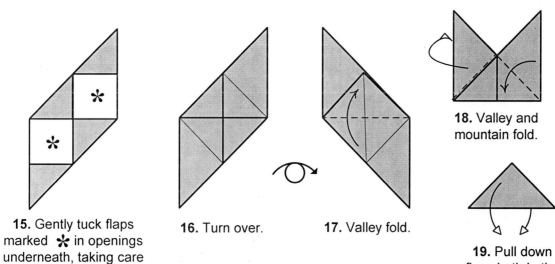

15. Gently tuck flaps marked ✳ in openings underneath, taking care not to rip paper.

16. Turn over.

17. Valley fold.

18. Valley and mountain fold.

19. Pull down flaps both in the front and back.

43

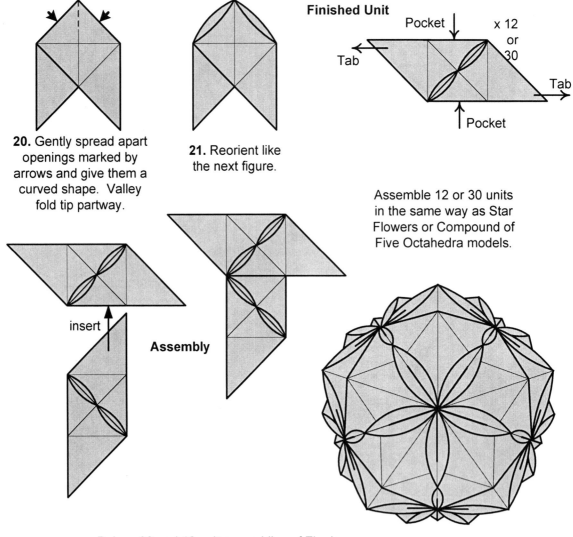

20. Gently spread apart openings marked by arrows and give them a curved shape. Valley fold tip partway.

21. Reorient like the next figure.

Finished Unit

Pocket

x 12 or 30

Tab

Tab

Pocket

Assemble 12 or 30 units in the same way as Star Flowers or Compound of Five Octahedra models.

insert

Assembly

Below: 30 and 12 unit assemblies of Zinnia.

Corolla

(Created July 2011)

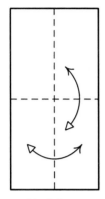

1. Start with 1:2 paper. Fold both book-folds and unfold.

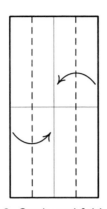

2. Cupboard fold.

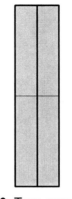

3. Turn over.

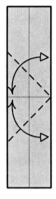

4. Valley fold and unfold at 45°.

5. Valley fold and unfold at 45°, then unfold all.

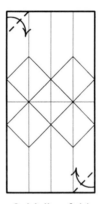

6. Valley fold corners.

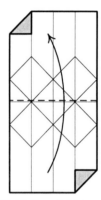

7. Valley fold pre-existing crease.

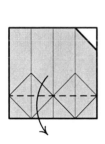

8. Valley fold as shown.

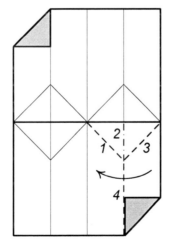

9. Valley and mountain fold following the sequence numbers. Folds *1* and *2* involve two layers.

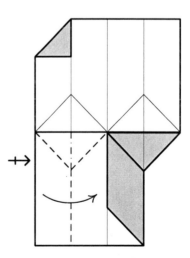

10. Repeat Step 9 on the left.

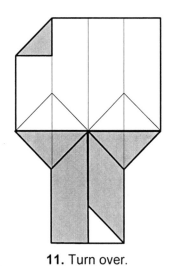

11. Turn over.

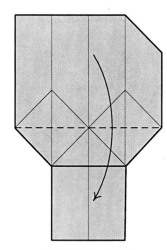

12. Valley fold.

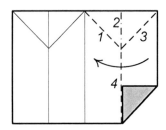

13. Repeat Step 9.

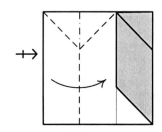

14. Repeat step 9 on the left.

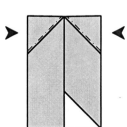

15. Reverse fold two corners. Make sure the folds go into the <u>center</u> of all layers.

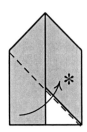

16. Valley fold top flap and tuck under ✱.

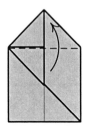

17. Valley fold top flap.

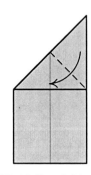

18. Valley fold.

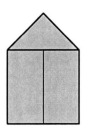

19. Turn over.

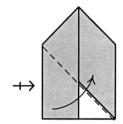

20. Repeat Steps 16–18.

21. Pull down flaps both in the front and back.

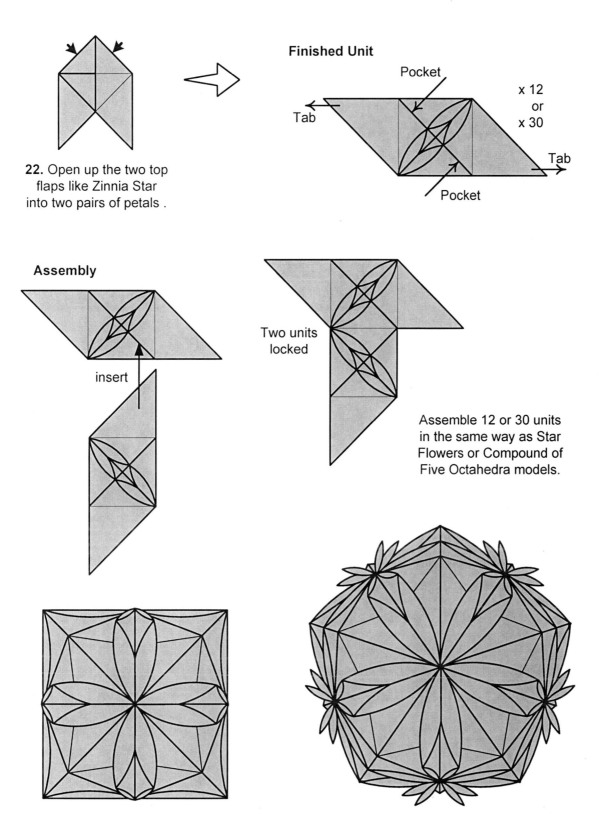

22. Open up the two top flaps like Zinnia Star into two pairs of petals .

Finished Unit

Pocket

Tab

x 12
or
x 30

Tab

Pocket

Assembly

insert

Two units locked

Assemble 12 or 30 units in the same way as Star Flowers or Compound of Five Octahedra models.

12-unit (left) and 30-unit (right) Corolla.

(Photos on cover and page 62)

Flower Star

(Created October 2010)

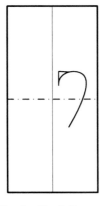

1. Start with 1:2 paper. Valley fold and unfold book-fold and then mountain fold into half.

2. Squash as shown.

3. Repeat behind.

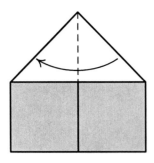

4. Valley fold top flap only.

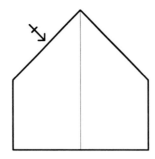

5. Repeat behind.

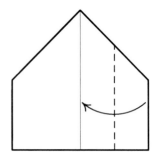

6. Valley fold, top flap only.

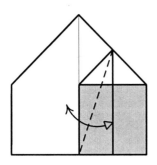

7. Valley fold and unfold, top flap only.

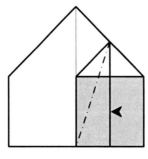

8. Inside reverse fold along crease you just made.

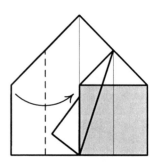

9. Valley fold, top flap only.

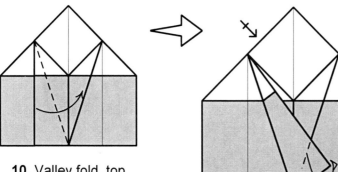

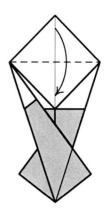

10. Valley fold, top flap only.

11. Mountain fold and unfold tip to trace edge at the back. Repeat all from Step 6 behind.

12. Valley fold to crease very firmly, then rotate 90°.

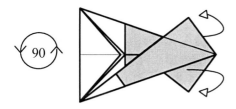

13. Pull tips apart gently to complete the unit.

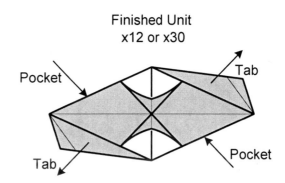

Finished Unit
x12 or x30

Pocket

Tab

Tab

Pocket

Assembly

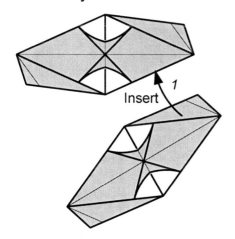

Insert *1*

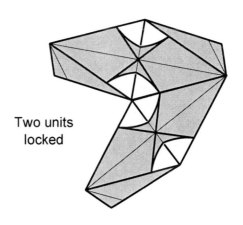

Two units locked

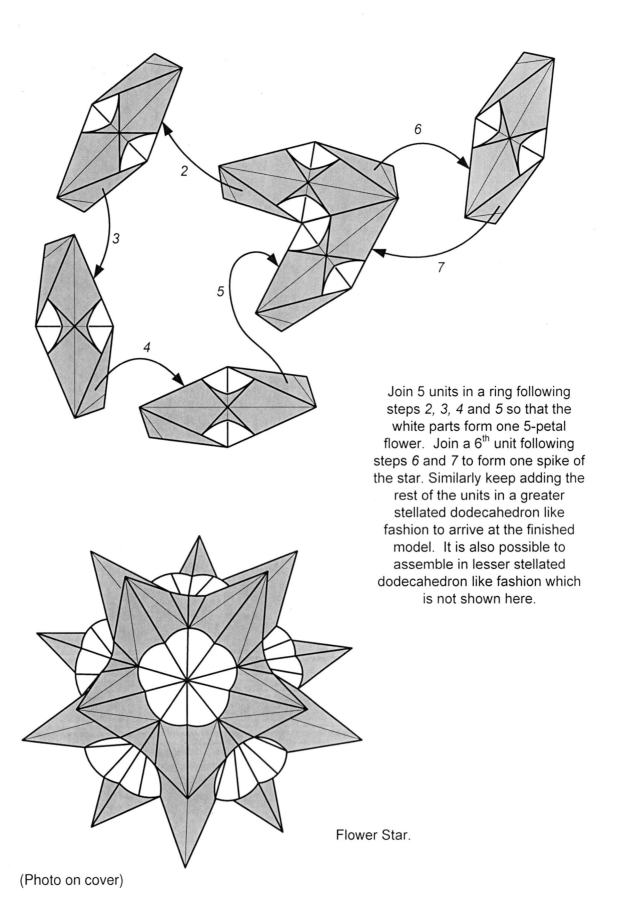

Join 5 units in a ring following steps 2, 3, 4 and 5 so that the white parts form one 5-petal flower. Join a 6th unit following steps 6 and 7 to form one spike of the star. Similarly keep adding the rest of the units in a greater stellated dodecahedron like fashion to arrive at the finished model. It is also possible to assemble in lesser stellated dodecahedron like fashion which is not shown here.

Flower Star.

(Photo on cover)

Flower Star Variation

(Created October 2010)

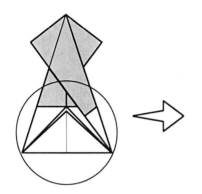

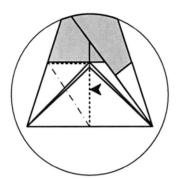

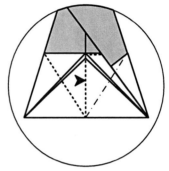

1. Start with Step 12 of previous model.

2. The dotted lines show inside flaps in X-ray vision. Inside reverse fold as shown. Repeat on the right flap and do Step 13 of previous model to complete unit.

Assemble exactly like Flower Star as explained in the previous page.

Finished Unit
x12 or x30

Pocket

Tab

Tab

Pocket

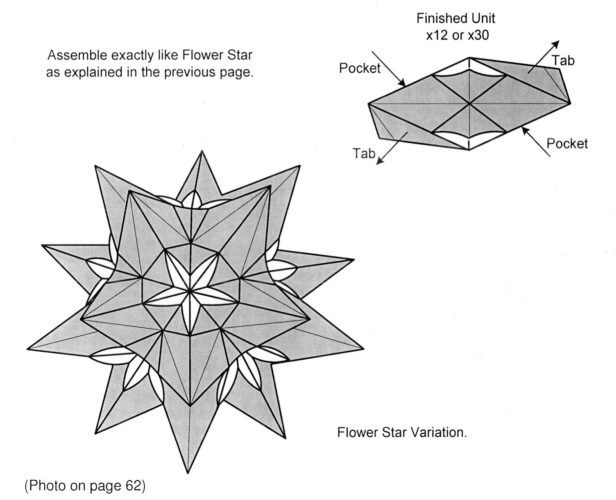

Flower Star Variation.

(Photo on page 62)

Zinnia Star

(Created October 2010)

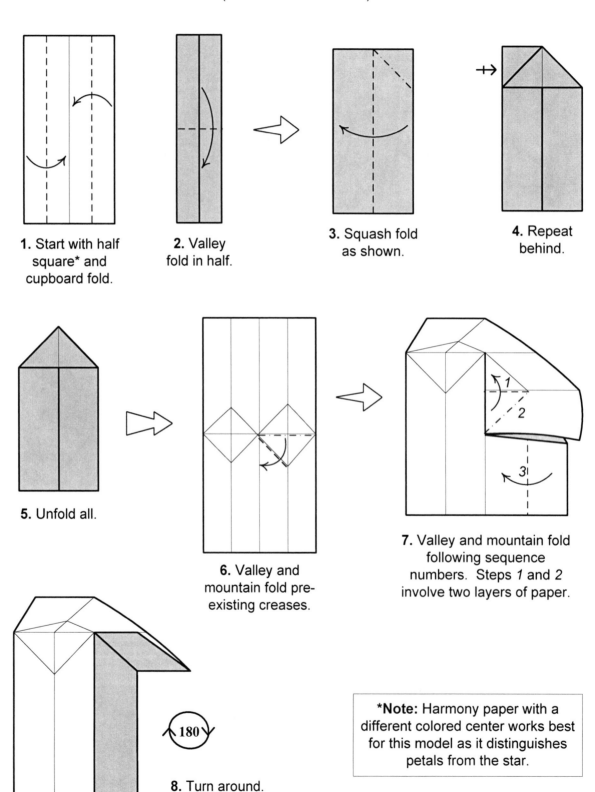

1. Start with half square* and cupboard fold.

2. Valley fold in half.

3. Squash fold as shown.

4. Repeat behind.

5. Unfold all.

6. Valley and mountain fold pre-existing creases.

7. Valley and mountain fold following sequence numbers. Steps *1* and *2* involve two layers of paper.

8. Turn around.

*Note: Harmony paper with a different colored center works best for this model as it distinguishes petals from the star.

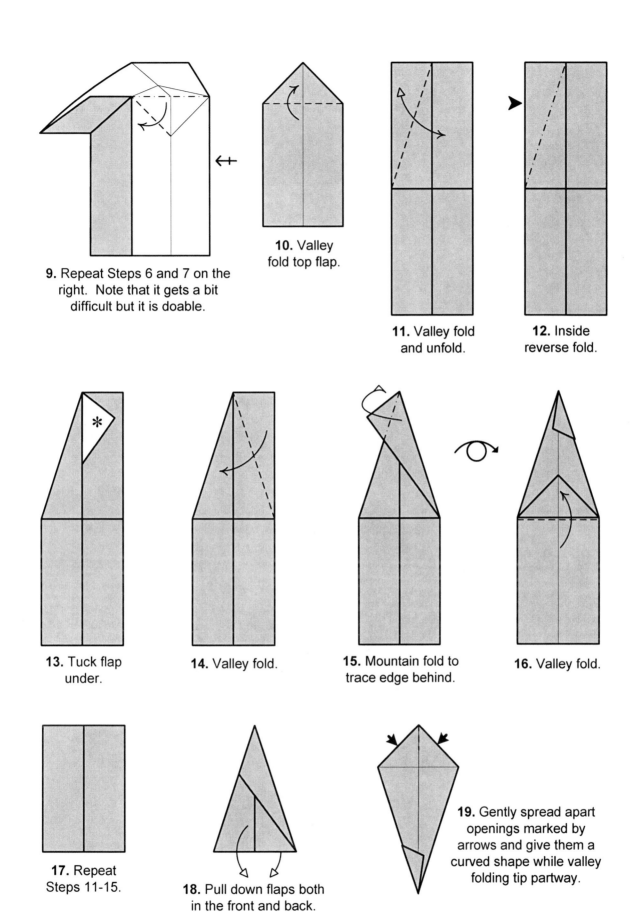

9. Repeat Steps 6 and 7 on the right. Note that it gets a bit difficult but it is doable.

10. Valley fold top flap.

11. Valley fold and unfold.

12. Inside reverse fold.

13. Tuck flap under.

14. Valley fold.

15. Mountain fold to trace edge behind.

16. Valley fold.

17. Repeat Steps 11-15.

18. Pull down flaps both in the front and back.

19. Gently spread apart openings marked by arrows and give them a curved shape while valley folding tip partway.

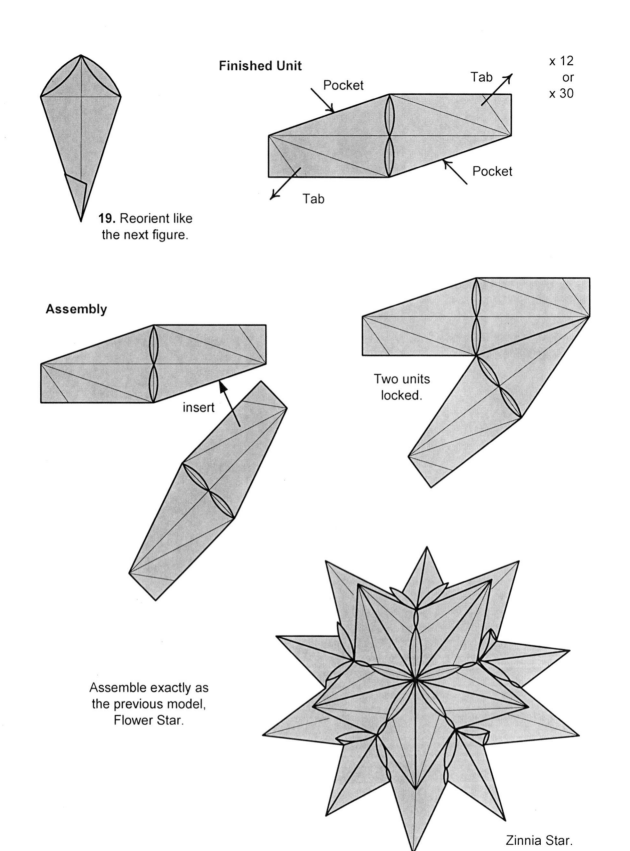

Finished Unit

Pocket

Tab

x 12
or
x 30

Tab

Pocket

19. Reorient like the next figure.

Assembly

insert

Two units locked.

Assemble exactly as the previous model, Flower Star.

Zinnia Star.

(Photo on back cover and alternate assembly photo on title page)

Corolla Star

(Created July 2011)

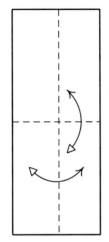

1. Start with 2:5 paper. Fold as shown.

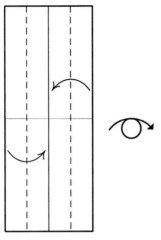

2. Cupboard fold and turn over.

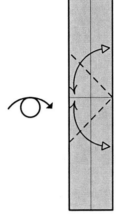

3. Valley fold and unfold as shown.

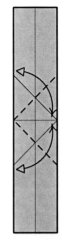

4. Valley fold and unfold, then unfold all.

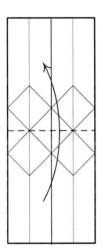

5. Valley fold at pre-existing crease.

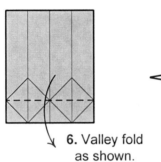

6. Valley fold as shown.

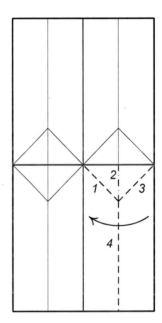

7. Valley and mountain fold following the sequence numbers. Folds *1* and *2* involve two layers.

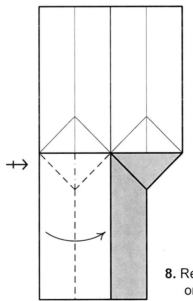

8. Repeat Step 7 on the left.

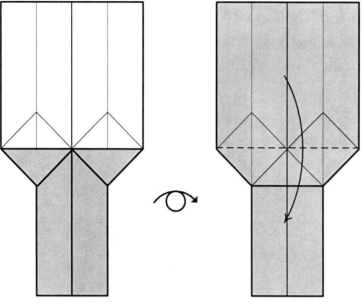

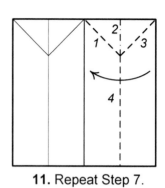

9. Turn over.

10. Valley fold.

11. Repeat Step 7.

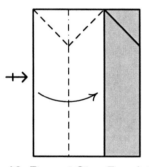

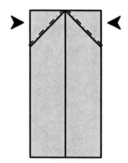

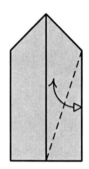

12. Repeat Step 7 on left.

13. Reverse fold two corners. Make sure the flaps end up in the <u>center</u> of all layers.

14. Valley fold and unfold top two layers only.

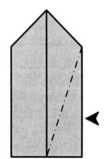

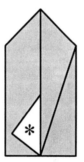

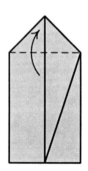

15. Inside reverse fold along crease just made.

16. Tuck white flap in layer underneath.

17. Valley fold top flap only.

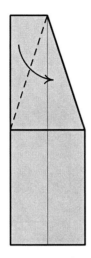

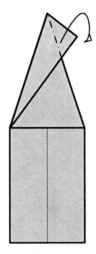

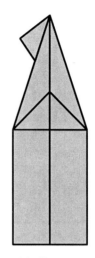

18. Valley fold as shown.

19. Mountain fold and unfold. Turn over.

20. Repeat Steps 14-19.

21. Unfold slightly and open up 4 petals as shown in Step 18 of previous model, Zinnia Star.

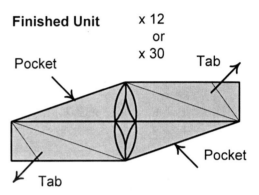

Finished Unit x 12 or x 30

Pocket

Tab

Pocket

Tab

Assembly
Assemble exactly like Flower Star. Try both lesser and greater stellated dodecahedron-like constructions.

Corolla Star.

(Photo on back cover)

Etna Kusudama

— Maria Sinayskaya (Created January 2011)

Making the template.

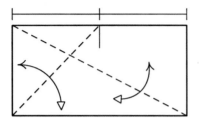
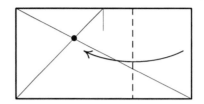
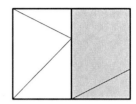

1. Start with half square and pinch midpoint. Fold and unfold the two diagonals shown.

2. Fold edge to where diagonals meet. This folds the rectangle into a third.

The complete template. Note that this method works for any rectangle.

Making the units.

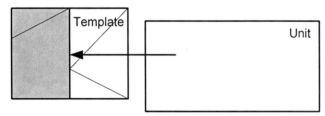
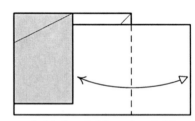

1. Start with same size half square as template. Orient template as shown and insert unit.

2. Valley fold and unfold as shown to get a third.

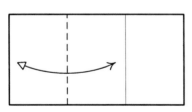
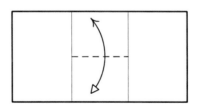
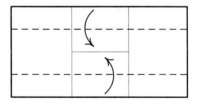

3. Valley fold and unfold as shown to get thirds.

4. Fold and unfold in half creasing middle section only.

5. Fold edges to new crease.

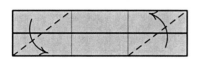
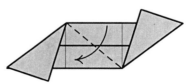

6. Fold the two diagonals shown.

7. Fold the diagonal of the middle section.

8. Valley and mountain fold along existing creases.

9. Unfold to Step 7.

Finished Unit

Pocket

Tab

Tab

Pocket

x6 or x12
or x30

Assembly (30 units)

insert

1

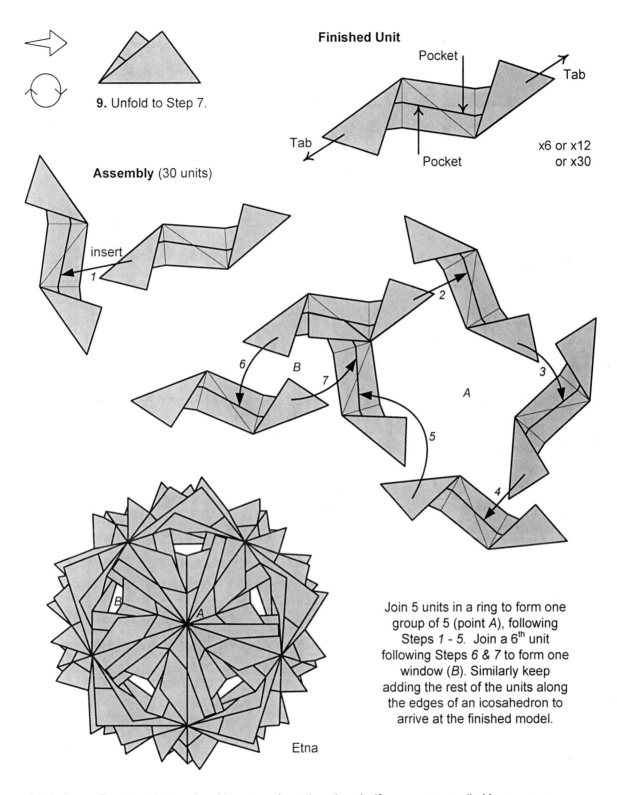

6

B

7

2

3

A

5

4

Join 5 units in a ring to form one
group of 5 (point *A*), following
Steps *1 - 5*. Join a 6th unit
following Steps *6 & 7* to form one
window (*B*). Similarly keep
adding the rest of the units along
the edges of an icosahedron to
arrive at the finished model.

Etna

Variations: Etna can be made with rectangles other than half squares as well. You can use
anything from 2:3 to 2:5 rectangles. The shorter the rectangles, the smaller the windows. At
boundary condition 2:3 you will get no windows and the model will look almost like a Sonobe
model. Any rectangle longer than aspect ratio 2:5 is not recommended.

(Photos on cover and page 62)

Helica Kusudama

— Ekaterina Lukasheva (Created June 2010)

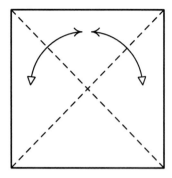

1. Fold and unfold both diagonals.

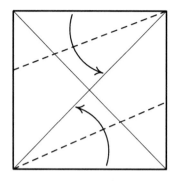

2. Bring edges to the diagonal shown.

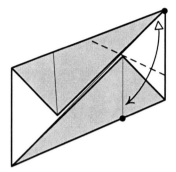

3. Fold to match dots and unfold.

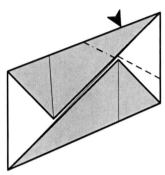

4. Inside reverse fold along crease just made.

5. Mountain fold corner as shown, creasing firmly.

6. Repeat Steps 3-5 on the left.

 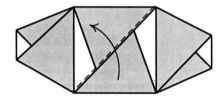

7. Valley fold.

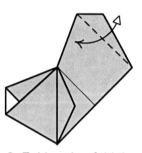

8. Fold and unfold tip.

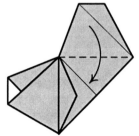

9. Valley fold.

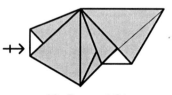

10. Repeat Steps 8 and 9 on left.

 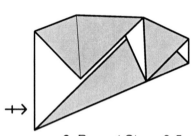

11. Unfold to Step 7 to complete unit.

Finished unit

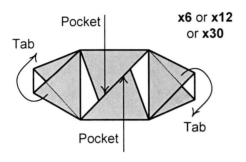

Pocket

Tab

x6 or **x12** or **x30**

Pocket

Tab

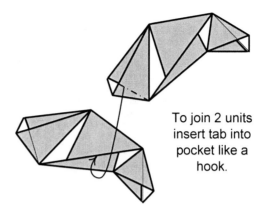

To join 2 units insert tab into pocket like a hook.

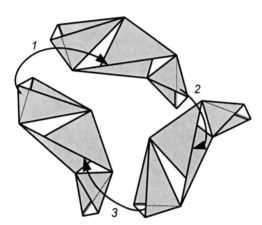

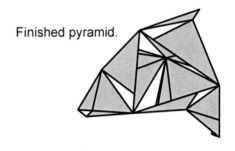

Finished pyramid.

Join 3 units following Steps *1*, *2* and *3* to form one stable pyramid. You can use these units to build structures based on various polyhedra by connecting 6, 12, 30 or more units just like Star Flower and Corolla. Note that the pyramid tips may be peeled down gently to bloom the model after assembly.

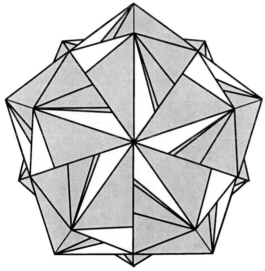

30-unit Helica before and after blooming.

(Photos on cover and page 62)

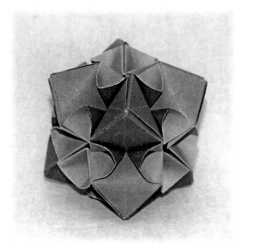 

12-unit assemblies of Star Flower (page 38) and Corolla (page 45).

Flower Star Variation (page 51) and Etna Variation with 2:3 rectangles (page 58).

Super Simple "Stellated" Cuboctahedron (page 15) and Unbloomed Helica (page 60).

Bibliography and Suggested Reading

[Bee01] Rick Beech, *Origami: The Complete Practical Guide to the Ancient Art of Paperfolding,* Lorenz Books, 2001.

[Bri11] Marcela Brina, *Contemporary Origami Decorations: Beautiful Modular Origami Projects to Enlighten your Life*, CreateSpace, 2011.

[Cox73] H. S. M. Coxeter, *Regular Polytopes*, Reprinted by Dover Publications, 1973.

[Dem07] Erik D. Demaine & Joseph O' Rourke, *Geometric Folding Algorithms, Linkages, Origami, Polyhedra*, Cambridge University Press, 2007.

[Dir97] Alexandra Dirk, *Origami Boxes for Gifts, Treasures and Trifles*, Sterling, 1997.

[Eng94] Peter Engel, *Origami from Angelfish to Zen*, Dover Publications, 1994.

[Eng11] Peter Engel, *Origami Odyssey: A Journey to the Edge of Paperfolding*, Tuttle Publishing, 2011.

[Fer07] Bruno Ferraz, *Ultrapassando Fronteiras com o Origami (Exceeding Borders with Origami)* (in Portugese), Editora Ciência Moderna, 2007.

[Fus89] Tomoko Fuse, *Origami Boxes*, Japan Publications Trading, 1989.

[Fus90] Tomoko Fuse, *Unit Origami: Multidimensional Transformations*, Japan Publications, 1990.

[Fus92] Tomoko Fuse, *Lets Fold Spirals,* Chikuma Shobo, 1992.

[Fus95] Tomoko Fuse, *Origami Spirals,* Chikuma Shobo, 1995.

[Fus96] Tomoko Fuse, *Joyful Origami Boxes*, Japan Publications Trading, 1996.

[Fus98] Tomoko Fuse, *Fabulous Origami Boxes*, Japan Publications Trading, 1998.

[Fus00] Tomoko Fuse, *Quick and Easy Origami Boxes*, Japan Publications Trading, 2000.

[Fus02] Tomoko Fuse, *Kusudama Origami*, Japan Publications Trading, 2002.

[Fus06] Tomoko Fuse, *Unit Polyhedron Origami,* Japan Publications Trading, 2006.

[Fus07] Tomoko Fuse, *Floral Origami Globes*, Japan Publications Trading, 2007.

[Fus10] Tomoko Fuse, *Unit Origami Essense*, Sun Trade Publishing, 2010.

[Fus10.1] Tomoko Fuse, *Unit Origami Fantasy*, Sun Trade Publishing, 2010.

[Gil07] Eduardo Gil Moré, *Papiroflexia Y Geometría* (in Spanish), Miguel A Salvatella, 2007.

[Gje08] Eric Gjerde, *Origami Tessellations: Awe-Inspiring Geometric Designs*, A K Peters/CRC, 2008.

[Gro05] Gay Merrill Gross, Ornagami: An Origami Christmas at Your Fingertips, Barnes & Noble, 2005.

[Gur95] Rona Gurkewitz and Bennett Arnstein, *3-D Geometric Origami: Modular Polyhedra*, Dover Publications, 1995.

[Gur99] Rona Gurkewitz, Bennett Arnstein, and Lewis Simon, *Modular Origami Polyhedra*, Dover Publications, 1999.

[Gur03] Rona Gurkewitz and Bennett Arnstein, *Multimodular Origami Polyhedra*, Dover Publications, 2003.

[Gur 08] Rona Gurkewitz, *Beginner's Book of Multimodular Origami Polyhedra: The Platonic Solids,* Dover Publications, 2008.

[Hul02] Thomas Hull, ed., *Origami 3: Third International Meeting of Origami Science, Mathematics, and Education,* A K Peters/CRC, 2002.

[Hul06] Thomas Hull, *Project Origami: Activities for Exploring Mathematics*, A K Peters/CRC, 2006.

[Jac87] Paul Jackson, *Encyclopedia of Origami/Papercraft Techniques*, Headline, 1987.

[Jac89] Paul Jackson, *Origami - A Complete Step-by-step Guide*, Hamlyn 1989.

[Kas98] Kunihiko Kasahara, *Origami for the Connoisseur*, Japan Publications, 1998.

[Kasa98] Kunihiko Kasahara, *Origami Omnibus: Paper Folding for Everybody*, Japan Publications, 1998.

[Kas03] Kunihiko Kasahara, *Extreme Origami*, Sterling, 2003.

[Kaw02] Miyuki Kawamura, *Polyhedron Origami for Beginners*, Japan Publications, 2002.

[Kawa01] Toshikazu Kawasaki, *Origami Dream World* (in Japanese), Asahipress, 2001.

[Kawa05] Toshikazu Kawasaki, *Roses, Origami & Math*, Japan Publications Trading, 2005.

[Kla09] Robert Klanten, *Papercraft: Design and Art With Paper*, Die Gestalten Verlag, 2009.

[Lan03] Robert Lang, *Origami Design Secrets: Mathematical Methods for an Ancient Art*, A K Peters/CRC, 2003.

[Lan08] Robert Lang, ed., *Origami 4: Fourth International Meeting of Origami Science, Mathematics, and Education*, A K Peters/CRC, 2008.

[Lan11] Robert Lang, *Twists, Tilings, and Tessellations*, A K Peters/CRC Press, 2011.

[Mit97] David Mitchell, *Mathematical Origami: Geometrical Shapes by Paper Folding*, Tarquin, 1997.

[Mit00] David Mitchell, *Paper Crystals: How to Make Enchanting Ornaments*, Water Trade, 2000.

[Mon09] John Montroll, *Origami Polyhedra Design*, A K Peters/CRC, Ltd., 2009.

[Muk07] Meenakshi Mukerji, *Marvelous Modular Origami*, A K Peters/CRC, 2007.

[Muk08] Meenakshi Mukerji, *Ornamental Origami: Exploring 3D Geometric Designs*, A K Peters/CRC, 2008.

[Muk10] Meenakshi Mukerji, *Origami Inspirations*, A K Peters/CRC, 2010.

[NOA94] NOA, *Minna Kusudama*, Nihon Origami Kyokai, 1994.

[Nol95] J. C. Nolan, Creating Origami, 1995.

[Ow96] Francis Ow, *Origami Hearts*, Japan Publications, 1996.

[Pet 98] David Petty,*Origami Wreaths and Rings*, Aitoh, 1998.

[Pet02] David Petty, *Origami 1-2-3*, Sterling, 2002.

[Pet06] David Petty, *Origami A-B-C*, Sterling, 2006.

[Rob04] Nick Robinson, *The Encyclopedia Of Origami*, Running Press, 2004.

[Row66] Tandalam Sundara Row, *Geometric Exercises in Paper Folding*, Reprinted by Dover Publications, 1966.

[Tan02] Origami Tanteidan,*Origami Tanteidan Convention No.8,* Origami House, 2002.

[Tem 86] Florence Temko, *Paper Pandas and Jumping Frogs,* China Books & Periodicals, 1986.

[Tem04] Florence Temko, *Origami Boxes and More*, Tuttle Publishing, 2004.

[Tub 06] Arnold Tubis and Crystal Mills, *Unfolding Mathematics with Origami Boxes*, Key Curriculum Press, 2006.

[Tub07] Arnold Tubis and Crystal Mills, *Fun with Folded Fabric Boxes*, C&T Publishing 2007.

[Wan11] Patsy Wang-Iverson, Robert Lang, Mark Yim, *Origami 5: Fifth International Meeting of Origami Science, Mathematics, and Education*, A K Peters/CRC, 2011.

[Yam90] Makoto Yamaguchi*, Kusudama Ball Origami*, Japan Publications, 1990.

Suggested Websites

Gilad Aharoni, *Gilad's Origami Page*, http://www.giladorigami.com/

Sara Adams, *Happy Folding*, http://www.happyfolding.com/

British Origami Society, *BOS Home Page*, http://britishorigami.info/

Krystyna & Wojtek Burczyk, *Burczyk Origami*, http://www1.zetosa.com.pl/~burczyk/origami/

George Hart, *The Pavilion of Polyhedreality*, http://www.georgehart.com/pavilion.html

Tom Hull, *Tom Hull's Home Page*, http://mars.wnec.edu/~th297133/origamimath.html

Japan Origami Academic Society, *Origami Tanteidan*, http://www.origami.gr.jp/index-e.html

Rachel Katz, *Origami with Rachel Katz*, http://www.origamiwithrachelkatz.com

Robert Lang, *Robert J. Lang Origami*, http://www.langorigami.com/

Ekaterina Lukasheva, *Kusudama me!,* http://kusudama.me/

David Mitchell, *Origami Heaven*, http://www.origamiheaven.com/

Meenakshi Mukerji, *Origami—MM's Modular Mania*, http://www.origamee.net/

Origami Resource Center, *Origami: the Art of Paper Folding*, http://www.origami-resource-center.com/index.html

Origami-USA, *Welcome to OrigamiUSA!*, http://origami-usa.org/

Francis Ow, *Francis Ow's Origami Page*, http://web.singnet.com.sg/~owrigami

David Petty, *Dave's Origami Emporium*, http://www.davidpetty.me.uk/

Jim Plank, *Jim Plank's Origami Page*, http://www.cs.utk.edu/~plank/plank/origami/

Halina Rosciszewska-Narloch, *Haligami World*, http://www.origami.friko.pl

Yuri & Katrin Shumakov, *Oriland*, http://www.oriland.com

Maria Sinayskaya, Flickr Photostream, http://www.flickr.com/photos/51642560@N02/

Helena Verrill, *Origami*, http://www.math.lsu.edu/~verrill/origami/

Paula Versnick, *Orihouse*, http://www.orihouse.com/

Dennis Walker, *Dennis Walker's Origami Page*, http://www.prospero78.freeserve.co.uk/

Dennis Walker, *Origami Database,* http://origamidatabase.com/

Joseph Wu, *Joseph Wu Origami,* http://www.origami.vancouver.bc.ca/

About The Author

2007, A K Peters published her first book, *Marvelous Modular Origami,* soon followed by her books *Ornamental Origami: Exploring 3D Geometric Designs* and *Origami Inspirations.* She has been a featured artist and a special guest at various origami conventions both in the US and abroad.

Meenakshi was born and raised in Kolkata, India. She obtained her BS in electrical engineering at the prestigious Indian Institute of Technology, Kharagpur, and then came to the United States to pursue a master's degree in computer science at Portland State University, Oregon. After successful completion of her studies, she joined the software industry and worked for more than a decade. She is now at home in California with her husband and two sons to enrich their lives, to create her own origami designs, and to author origami books. People who have provided her with much origami inspiration and encouragement are Rosalinda Sanchez, David Petty, Francis Ow, Rona Gurkewitz, Robert Lang, Rachel Katz, Ravi Apte, and the numerous visitors of her website.

Meenakshi Mukerji (Adhikari) was introduced to origami in early childhood by her uncle Bireshwar Mukhopadhyay. She rediscovered origami in its modular form as an adult quite by chance in 1995, when she was living in Pittsburgh, PA. She attended a modular origami class taught by Doug Philips and ever since she has been folding modular origami and displaying it on her very popular website www.origamee.net. In 2005, Origami USA presented her with the Florence Temko award for generously sharing her origami work on her website. In April

Guest Contributors

Dennis Walker (UK), Maria Sinayskaya (Russia), and Ekaterina Lukasheva (Russia).
(Please be sure to visit their websites listed in *Suggested Websites* on previous page.)

Author's other Books

| 2007 | 2008 | 2010 |

Meenakshi Mukerji's books have received rave reviews from various origami and mathematical societies worldwide. Her books have been praised by Origami USA, British Origami Society, Polish Origami Association, MAA Reviews, London Mathematical Society, Science News, Zentralblatt Math, Mathematics teaching in Middle School and many other societies. Additionally, she has contributed diagrams and articles to numerous other origami books and periodicals.

Author's Website

Meenakshi's Modular Mania, (http://www.origamee.net): Maintained by the author since 1997 until present, colorful and vibrant, the website features photo galleries of her own works as well as others' works folded by her. You'll also find a large collection of diagrams of some of her designs and links to diagrams of other people's designs. It is one of the top websites for "modular origami" worldwide web search and has had over a million hits. Many regular visitors have left wonderful comments on her guestbook about how useful the site is and how it has helped them in school or college projects. Some have also noted that they have found making the art presented on the website to be very therapeutic and relaxing. One has expressed that the site is so powerful that it has "proselytized" him from regular origami to modular origami. To end the book here is a quote from the website's guest book by Anindya Banerjee, a journalist from New Delhi, India: "... I never knew one could create sheer poetry on paper without letting a drop of ink touch it".

CPSIA information can be obtained at www.ICGtesting.com
Printed in the USA
BVOW051213190212

283266BV00007B/3/P

9 781463 707606